SIGMA
Memory Jogger™ II

A Pocket Guide of Tools for Six Sigma Improvement Teams

Michael Brassard
Brassard & Ritter, LLC

Lynda Finn
Oriel Inc.

Dana Ginn
Oriel Inc.

Diane Ritter
Brassard & Ritter, LLC

First Edition
GOAL/QPC

The Six Sigma Memory Jogger™ II

© 1994, 2002 by GOAL/QPC
All rights reserved.

Reproduction of any part of this publication without the written permission of GOAL/QPC is prohibited.

Six Sigma is a federally registered trademark of Motorola, Inc.

Cathy Kingery, *Editor*
Deborah Crovo, Judi Glidden, Michele Kierstead, *Graphics*
Michele Kierstead, *Cover Design, Layout*
Bob Page, *Project Manager, GOAL/QPC*
Christine Jersild, *Project Manager, Oriel Inc.*

GOAL/QPC

12B Manor Parkway, Salem, NH 03079-2862
800-643-4316 **or** 603-893-1944
Fax: 603-870-9122
E-mail: service@goalqpc.com
Web site: www.goalqpc.com

Printed in the United States of America

First Edition   10 9 8 7 6 5 4 3 2

ISBN 1-57681-044-5

Acknowledgments

Our thanks and gratitude go to the people and organizations who offered encouragement and suggestions for this book or who gave us permission to use their examples, graphs, and charts.

Special thanks to Patricia Klossner, president of Oriel Inc., who generously and graciously enabled us to access the wealth of experience she and her team have gained in working to develop Six Sigma leaders and team members. Since 1995, when we collaborated to produce *The Team Memory Jogger*™, Pat has been a model partner and a great friend.

Thanks also to Kristi Brown, *Wal-Mart*; and Ruth Fattori, *Conseco Inc.*, who reviewed and critiqued draft copy to ensure that the book met their expectations, and to everyone who helped with the original *Memory Jogger*™ *II*:

Bryce Colburne, *AT&T Technologies*; Robert Brodeur, *Bell Canada*; Karen Tate, *BGP*; Rip Stauffer, *BlueFire Partners*; Weston F. Milliken, *CUE Consulting*; Raymond A. Kach, *Ford Motor Company*; Paula McIntosh, *Georgia State Dept. of Human Resources, Division of Rehabilitation Services*; Donald Botto, *Goodyear Tire & Rubber Company*; Tony Borgen and Paul Hearn, *Hamilton Standard*; Lloyd S. Nelson, *Nashua Corp.*; Jack Waddell, *Novacor Chemicals*; Kirk Kochenberger, *Parkview Episcopal Medical Center*; Marie Sinioris, *Rush-Presbyterian-St. Luke's Medical Center*; Tim Barnes, *Smith-Kline Beecham*; Dennis Crowley, *St. John Fisher College*; Buzz Stapczynski, *Town of Andover, MA*; Kemper Watkins, MSgt., *U.S. Air Force, Air Combat Command*; Capt. T. C. Splitgerber, *U.S. Navy, Naval Dental Center, San Diego, CA*.

Foreword

Published in 1994, the original *Memory Jogger™ II* introduced many of the quality tools commonly used for process improvement, planning, and problem solving, but it lacked specific information on how and when these tools should be used in support of Six Sigma.

In the late 1990s, many leading Six Sigma organizations began asking us to create customized versions of *The Memory Jogger™ II*. In additon to the quality tools, these books also contained company-specific Six Sigma material. In time, we concluded that a widespread need existed that would be met if we created *The Six Sigma Memory Jogger™ II*.

To that end, we enlisted the help of Oriel Inc. of Madison, Wisconsin, to ensure that this book's content is appropriate for Six Sigma team members. Oriel has extensive experience in training and coaching Six Sigma teams and project leaders.

We believe that the insights contained in this book, which we have gathered from many sources, combine to create a valuable resource for helping Six Sigma teams to learn and apply these powerful quality tools. We trust you will agree.

Bob Page
GOAL/QPC

Table of Contents

Six Sigma Overview	1
DMAIC	11
Activity Network Diagram (AND)	27
Affinity Diagram	38
Brainstorming	45
Cause & Effect/Fishbone Diagram	49
Charter	59
Commitment Scale	67
Communication Plan	70
Control Charts	75
Critical To Quality (CTQ) Tree	91
Data Collection	95
Data Points	101
Design of Experiments (DOE)	105
Failure Mode and Effects Analysis (FMEA)	111
Flowchart	116
Focused Problem Statement	124
Histogram	129
Stratifying Frequency Diagrams	139
Box Plot	140
Hypothesis Testing	142
Interrelationship Digraph	147
Involvement Matrix	156
Kano Model	158
Matrix Diagram	162

Measurement Systems Analysis (MSA)	168
Operational Definitions	176
Pareto Chart	178
Pareto Chart Stratification	182
Prioritization Matrices	189
Process Management Chart	199
Process Sigma	204
Regression	214
Run Chart	221
Scatter Diagram	228
SIPOC	235
Six Sigma Storyboard	239
Taguchi Loss Function	244
Tollgate Review	247
Tree Diagram	249
Voice of the Customer (VOC) Data-Collection System	258
$y = f(x)$ Formula	263

Six Sigma Overview

What is Six Sigma?

Sigma is a statistical concept that represents the amount of variation present in a process relative to customer requirements or specifications. When a process operates at the six sigma level, the variation is so small that the resulting products and services are 99.9997% defect free.

"Six Sigma" is commonly denoted in several different ways. You might see it written as "6σ," "6 Sigma," or "6s."

In addition to being a statistical measure of variation, the term *Six Sigma* also refers to a business philosophy of focusing on continuous improvement by understanding customers' needs, analyzing business processes, and instituting proper measurement methods. Furthermore, it is a methodology that an organization uses to ensure that it is improving its key processes.

While Six Sigma corresponds to being 99.9997% defect free, not all business processes need to attain this high a goal. Companies can also use the Six Sigma methodology to identify which of their key business processes would benefit most from improvement and then focus their improvement efforts there.

In this book, we often use the more generic terms *sigma* or *process sigma* to refer to the current capability of a process (i.e., how well the process is performing relative to customer specifications).

Process Capability

Amount of Variation	Effect	Sigma Value
Too much	Hard to produce output within customer requirements or specifications	Low (0–2)
Moderate	Most output meets customer requirements	Middle (2–4.5)
Very little	Virtually all output meets customer requirements (less than four parts per million not meeting specifications)	High (4.5–6)

To increase your organization's process-sigma level, you must decrease the amount of variation that occurs. Having less variation gives you the following benefits:

- Greater predictability in the process.
- Less waste and rework, which lowers costs.
- Products and services that perform better and last longer.
- Happier customers who value you as a supplier.

The simple example below illustrates the concept of Six Sigma. Note that the amount of data in this example is limited, but it serves to describe the concept adequately.

Two companies deliver pizza to your house. You want to determine which one can better meet your needs. You always want your pizza delivered at 6 p.m. but are willing to tolerate a delivery anytime between 5:45 p.m. and 6:15 p.m. In this example, the target is 6 p.m. and the customer specifications are 5:45 p.m. on the low side and 6:15 p.m. on the high side.

You decide to order two pizzas at the same time every night for ten days—one pizza from Company A, and one from Company B. You track the delivery times for ten days and collect the following data:

Comparison of Delivery Times

Company A		Company B	
Day	Delivery Time	Day	Delivery Time
1	5:58	1	5:51
2	6:20	2	6:04
3	5:49	3	5:59
4	6:05	4	6:00
5	6:10	5	6:10
6	5:42	6	5:56
7	6:01	7	6:02
8	5:53	8	6:11
9	6:12	9	5:59
10	6:05	10	6:09

As the chart above shows, Company A had two occurrences—on Day 2 and Day 6—of pizza arrival times that were outside of your tolerance window of between 5:45 and 6:15. In Six Sigma terminology, these two occurrences are called *defects*. This performance can also be described visually with the following graphs:

Defects and Variation

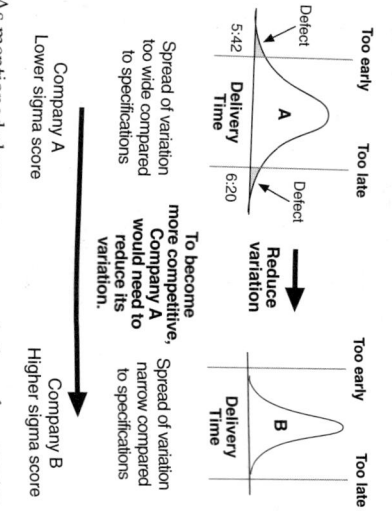

```
         Too early        Too late              Too early        Too late
              Defect                                  
                  [curve A]                              [curve B]
                                        Defect
         5:42              6:20
              Delivery                              Delivery
                Time                                  Time

         Company A                              Company B
     Lower sigma score                       Higher sigma score
```

Spread of variation too wide compared to specifications

To become more competitive, Company A would need to reduce its variation.

Reduce variation →

Spread of variation narrow compared to specifications

As mentioned above, a process variation of no greater than Six Sigma is equivalent to being 99.9997% defect free. Although a 99.9% defect-free level of quality (which is equivalent to a sigma level greater than four) sounds adequate, in a world operating at this sigma level, the following situations would occur:

- At least 20,000 wrong drug prescriptions dispensed per year.
- Unsafe drinking water for almost one hour a month.
- No telephone service or television transmission for nearly ten minutes each week.
- Ninety-six crashes per 100,000 airline flights.

Experts believe that the quality levels for most businesses today fall within the three- to four-sigma range.

Six Sigma terminology

Organizations that adopt a Six Sigma philosophy and methodology employ a commonly used and understood its pioneering work, Motorola holds the trademark for the Six Sigma® methodology.

During the mid-1980s, Motorola joined forces with several other companies, including ABB (Asea Brown Boveri), AlliedSignal, Kodak, IBM, and Texas Instruments, to found the Six Sigma Research Institute. This effort began the expansion and commercialization of the process of achieving Six Sigma capability.

The Six Sigma concept and methods have gained popularity in part due to publicity about former General Electric CEO Jack Welch's commitment to achieving Six Sigma capability.

Why should I use Six Sigma?

The benefits of following the Six Sigma concept and using the accompanying methods are many. They include the following:

- Having a measurable way to track performance improvements.
- Focusing your attention on process management at all organizational levels.
- Improving your customer relationships by addressing defects.
- Improving the efficiency and effectiveness of your processes by aligning them with your customers' needs.

Conducting measurable tracking keeps you informed about what changes are working and which ones are not. It can also speed up significant improvement. Having a process focus lets you define defects and calculate sigma levels. Aligning a process with your customers' needs can result in greater customer loyalty and retention. Also, by being in touch with your customers and their needs, you can more easily

6 Six Sigma Overview ©2002 GOAL/QPC

vocabulary. These terms are used frequently throughout this book, and you will use them often as you work on your organization's sigma improvement teams. Below is a sampling of these terms.

Critical To Quality (CTQ) characteristic: A key feature by which customers evaluate the quality of your product or service and that can be used as measures for your project. A useful CTQ characteristic has the following features:

- It is critical to the customer's perception of quality.
- It can be measured.
- A specification can be set to tell whether the CTQ characteristic has been achieved.

unit: An item that you produce or process.

defect: Any unit or event that does not meet customer requirements. A defect must be measurable.

defective: A unit with one or more defects.

defect opportunity: A measurable chance for a defect to occur.

sigma: An expression of process yield based on the number of defects per million opportunities, or DPMO.

Where, why, and how did Six Sigma begin?

The Six Sigma philosophy and methodology started at Motorola Corporation in the mid-1980s, when the company discovered that products with a high first-pass yield (i.e., those that made it through the production process defect-free) rarely failed in actual use. Motorola began focusing on creating strategies to reduce defects in its products and in 1988 was among the first group of organizations to win the Malcolm Baldrige National Quality Award. Today, based on

©2002 GOAL/QPC   Six Sigma Overview 5

develop new ideas for improvements and enhancements to your products and services.

How does Six Sigma differ from Continuous Quality Improvement (CQI)?

Although some Six Sigma concepts and tools are similar to those used for CQI, Six Sigma emphasizes the following points:

- An increased focus on quality as defined by your customers. The sigma score directly addresses this issue.
- More rigorous statistical methods.
- Prioritization of your improvement projects and alignment of your resources to support your organization's key strategic initiatives.

If you are familiar with CQI, you are probably already familiar with some of the tools described in this book. But you will also find some new tools that you can add to your Six Sigma tool belt.

If you are not already familiar with CQI, then you will learn many new tools that will help you improve the effectiveness of your organization's processes and their ability to meet your customers' needs.

What is needed for a successful Six Sigma program?

Your process-sigma work will be successful only if your organization has an environment that supports its continued and consistent use. To accomplish this, your organization should do the following:

- Have management lead your improvement efforts.
- Actively support a focus on delighting your customers.

- Provide the sigma improvement team with access to experts who can offer ongoing guidance and coaching.
- Encourage open discussion about defects. People should not be afraid to point out that something is wrong. The airline industry, for instance, studies crashes and "near-misses" to improve safety.
- Value and use the data you gather.
- Help employees work effectively by providing a team-based, cooperative environment.

What are the Six Sigma methodologies?

There are two basic methodologies introduced in Six Sigma organizations. They are known by their acronyms: DMAIC and DMADV.

The DMAIC method involves five steps: **D**efine, **M**easure, **A**nalyze, **I**mprove, and **C**ontrol. This method is used to improve the current capabilities of an existing process. This is by far the most commonly used methodology of sigma improvement teams and is described in detail in the next section of this book.

In the DMAIC method, the CTQs are defined first. The improvement team then studies each one intensively to understand the key drivers that influence successful process performance. Improvements in the key drivers can then be made, and the process can attain the required Six Sigma level and thereby meet the CTQs.

The Five Steps of the DMAIC Method

The five steps of the DMAIC method are outlined below.

1. Define the project.
- Define the project's purpose and scope.
- Collect background information on the process and your customers' needs and requirements.

2. Measure the current situation.
- Gather information on the current situation to provide a clearer focus for your improvement effort.

3. Analyze to identify causes.
- Identify the root causes of defects.
- Confirm them with data.

4. Improve.
- Develop, try out, and implement solutions that address the root causes.
- Use data to evaluate results for the solutions and the plans used to carry them out.

5. Control.
- Maintain the gains that you have achieved by standardizing your work methods or processes.
- Anticipate future improvements and make plans to preserve the lessons learned from this improvement effort.

The DMAIC method is very robust. Many organizations have used it successfully to produce dramatic improvements. Using the DMAIC method also results in the following benefits:

- It provides a framework.
- It provides a common language.
- It provides a checklist to prevent skipping critical steps in the process.
- It enables you to improve the way in which you improve.

Note: Some organizations use the RDMAIC method, in which a **R**ecognize step is added to the beginning of the improvement process. This step involves using techniques to identify the most urgent projects to work on and/or the ones that will result in the greatest benefit to the organization and its customers.

The DMADV method is used when you need to create a process, product, or service to meet customer requirements or when you need a complete redesign because the process, product, or service is consistently incapable of meeting customer requirements. This method is much less frequently used than the DMAIC method. DMADV teams are usually convened and staffed by senior managers. While many of this method's tools and processes are the same as for DMAIC, others are typically performed only by Six Sigma Experts. These tools are beyond the scope of this book.

Like the DMAIC method, the DMADV method involves five steps: **D**efine, **M**easure, **A**nalyze, **D**esign, and **V**erify. In this method, the improvement team defines the CTQs first. The team then creates a product, service, or process that optimizes performance so it satisfies the critical CTQs.

DMAIC

As a Six Sigma team member, you will most likely work on improvement teams using the DMAIC method. To use this method successfully, you must first be familiar with the goals and outputs of each step, as well as the correct approach to take during each step and the tools necessary to complete your work.

The DMAIC Process Flow

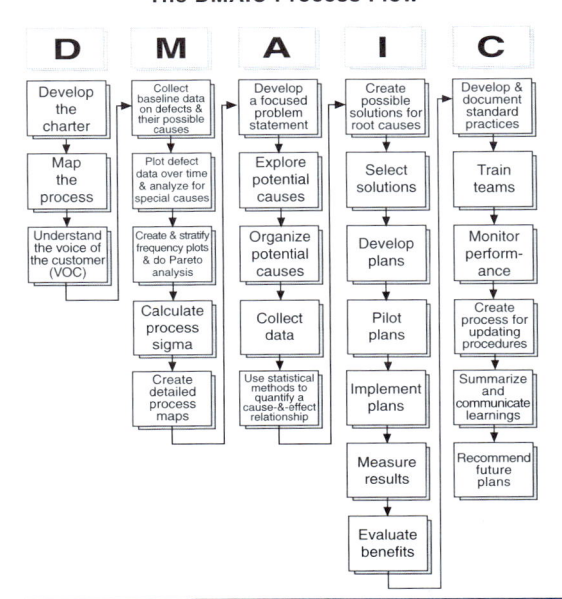

D
- Develop the charter
- Map the process
- Understand the voice of the customer (VOC)

M
- Collect baseline data on defects & their possible causes
- Plot defect data over time & analyze for special causes
- Create & stratify frequency plots & do Pareto analysis
- Calculate process sigma
- Create detailed process maps

A
- Develop a focused problem statement
- Explore potential causes
- Organize potential causes
- Collect data
- Use statistical methods to quantify a cause-&-effect relationship

I
- Create possible solutions for root causes
- Select solutions
- Develop plans
- Pilot plans
- Implement plans
- Measure results
- Evaluate benefits

C
- Develop & document standard practices
- Train teams
- Monitor performance
- Create process for updating procedures
- Summarize and communicate learnings
- Recommend future plans

©2002 GOAL/QPC

The goals, outputs, approach, and tools for each step of the DMAIC method are outlined on the next several pages.

The Define Step

Goals and outputs

The goal of the Define step is to define the project's purpose and scope and obtain background information about the process and its customers.

The outputs of the Define step consist of the following:

- A clear statement of the intended improvement and how you will measure it.
- A high-level map of the process.
- A translation of the voice of the customer, or VOC (see page 258 for details), into key quality characteristics.

Approach

The "Define Step" Process Flow

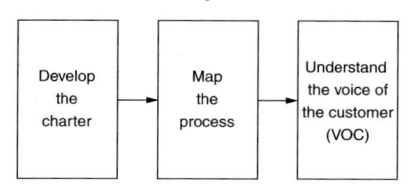

```
Develop         Map            Understand
the      →     the       →    the voice of
charter       process         the customer
                                  (VOC)
```

To fully define the scope and purpose of your project, you must first understand the boundaries of the process you are trying to improve and the requirements of its customers. You include this information, along with expected resource needs and a projected timeline, in your team charter.

In practice, there is usually some give and take between these activities as you work to define a project that is both important and doable.

The applicable tools for the Define step include the following:

Tool	Description	Page
Affinity Diagram	Enables your team to organize and summarize language-based data.	38
Charter	Documents what the project is supposed to achieve and what resources are available to your team. A written charter is an important communication and reference tool.	59
Communication Plan	Regular communication with stakeholders (i.e., people who will be affected by the project or can influence it but are not directly involved with doing the project work) can help your team understand its work, identify better solutions to problems, create more buy-in, understand when and how to best involve others, and avoid pitfalls.	70
Control Charts	Focus attention on detecting and monitoring process variation over time.	75
CTQ Tree	Critical To Quality (CTQ) characteristics are features by which customers evaluate the quality of your product or service. The CTQ Tree enables your team to describe your customers' needs and the corresponding measurable characteristics. If a product or service does not meet a CTQ, it is considered to be defective.	91
Data Collection	Data from customers helps your team understand what's important about your project and set priorities if you need to narrow the project's scope. Often the necessary customer data is provided to a team when it is formed.	95

Continued on the next page

Tool	Description	Page
Kano Model	Helps your team understand your customers' requirements, which are sorted into three categories: Must Be, More Is Better, and Delighters.	158
Pareto Chart	Helps your team focus its efforts on the problems that are causing the most trouble. This helps you identify the areas where your efforts will have the biggest payback.	178
Run Chart	Enables your team to study baseline process performance to identify trends or patterns over time.	221
SIPOC	A SIPOC (Suppliers, Inputs, Process, Outputs, and Customers) analysis helps your team understand the key elements of your process and define the boundaries and scope for your project.	235
Tollgate Review	A formal review process that helps keep the project on track and helps promote successful results.	247
$y = f(x)$ Formula	Allows your team to structure the relationship among the Y's (the CTQs), the y's (the process outputs directly affecting the Y's), and the x's (the causal factors directly affecting the y's).	263

The Measure Step

Goals and outputs

The goal of the Measure step is to focus your improvement effort by gathering information about the current situation.

The outputs of the Measure step include the following:

- Data that pinpoints the problem's location or rate of occurrence.

- Baseline data on how well the process meets customer needs (to determine the current process sigma).
- An understanding of how the current process operates.
- A more focused problem statement.

Approach

The "Measure Step" Process Flow

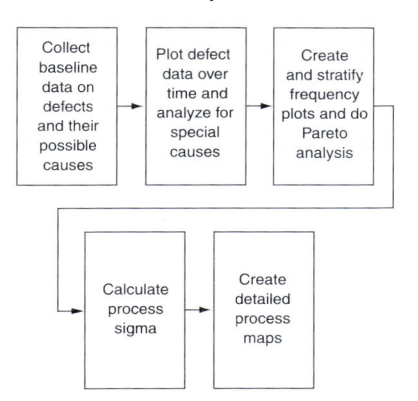

```
Collect baseline    →  Plot defect data      →  Create and stratify
data on defects        over time and            frequency plots and
and their possible     analyze for special      do Pareto analysis
causes                 causes
                                                        ↓
                       Calculate          ←    Create detailed
                       process sigma           process maps
```

During the Measure step, you investigate the problem you are studying in detail—what specifically is happening, when it is happening, and where it is happening. You also collect data to create a performance baseline to which you can compare the process performance after you work on the Improve step.

The applicable tools for the Measure step include the following:

Tool	Description	Page
Control Charts	Help you look for patterns over time in process variation, quantify the current capability of your process, and identify when special events interrupt normal operations.	75
Data Collection	Helps you systematically collect baseline data.	95
Data Points/ Data Types	The type of data you have will determine which tool(s) to use.	101
Flowchart	Pinpoints steps in the process that don't add value and helps you identify problems in the process that contribute to waste and defects.	116
Histogram	Reveals how often a problem occurs in different settings. A stratified Histogram helps you identify process characteristics that might provide clues about the potential causes of problems.	129
Measurement Systems Analysis (MSA)	Helps you understand measurement variation.	168
Operational Definitions	Precise descriptions that describe how to get a value for each characteristic you are trying to measure.	176
Pareto Chart	Displays the relative importance of problems. As in the Define step, it helps you focus your attention and develop a detailed problem statement.	178
Process Sigma	Calculations that describe the current process capability. Calculating a baseline process-sigma level provides a gauge for you to evaluate your progress.	204
Run Chart	Plots data from Check Sheets and other sources and helps you look for patterns over time in process variation.	221

Continued on the next page

Tool	Description	Page
Taguchi Loss Function	Defines the loss associated with variation around a customer-specification target.	244
Tollgate Review	A formal review process that helps keep the project on track and helps promote successful results.	247

The Analyze Step

Goals and outputs

The goal of the Analyze step is to identify root causes and confirm them with data. The output of this step is a theory that you have tested and confirmed.

Approach

The "Analyze Step" Process Flow

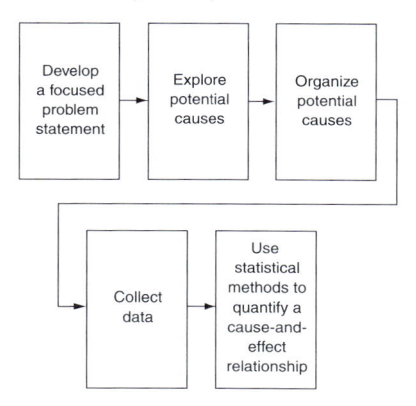

Develop a focused problem statement → Explore potential causes → Organize potential causes → Collect data → Use statistical methods to quantify a cause-and-effect relationship

The Analyze step pinpoints the specific cause(s) of the focused problem statement you will develop as a result of the Measure step. You can then address the root cause(s) through solutions you implement in the Improve step.

The applicable tools for the Analyze step include the following:

Tool	Description	Page
Brainstorming	Enables your team to creatively and efficiently generate a large number of ideas about causes of error.	45
Cause-and-Effect Diagram	Enables your team to identify, explore, and graphically display, in increasing detail, all the possible causes related to a problem. The deeper you are able to push for causes, the more likely your solutions will be long-lasting ones.	49
Design of Experiments (DOE)	Provides a method for testing multiple potential causes of error at the same time, enabling your team to reach conclusions about the primary causes.	105
Focused Problem Statement	Describes specifically what occurs, when or under what circumstances it occurs, and/or who is involved. The goal is to narrow the problem definition so you can use your time and resources most effectively to find a solution.	124
Histogram	Stratified Histograms help you identify process characteristics that might confirm patterns. Like Scatter Diagrams, they help you understand relationships that can confirm an underlying cause of a problem.	129
Hypothesis Testing	Using statistical analysis on a cause-and-effect relationship.	142

Continued on the next page

Tool	Description	Page
Interrelationship Digraph (ID)	Studying cause-and-effect patterns to identify the key drivers and outcomes of critical issues.	147
Scatter Diagram	Used to show the relationship between two variables. It can help your team verify causal relationships.	228
Tollgate Review	A formal review process that helps keep the project on track and helps promote successful results.	247
Tree Diagram	Breaks down the broad categories of causes into increasing levels of detail. Your team can use it to depict the links between root causes and their effects on a problem.	249

The Improve Step

Goals and outputs

The goal of the Improve step is to develop, try out, and implement solutions that address root causes and to use data to evaluate the solutions as well as the plans you use to carry them out.

The outputs of the Improve step include the following:

- Planned, tested actions that eliminate or reduce the impact of the identified root cause(s) of a problem.
- "Before" and "after" data analysis that shows how much of the initial gap was closed.
- A comparison of the plan to the actual implementation.

Approach

The "Improve Step" Process Flow

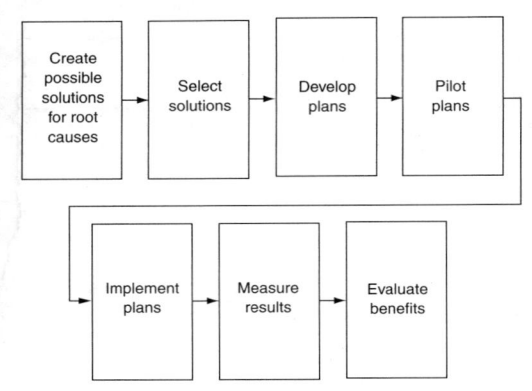

Create possible solutions for root causes → Select solutions → Develop plans → Pilot plans → Implement plans → Measure results → Evaluate benefits

The Improve step involves not only coming up with solutions but also using the PDCA (Plan-Do-Check-Act) Cycle to evaluate and improve the solutions you want to implement. Preparing people for change is another critical component of this step.

The applicable tools for the Improve step include the following:

Tool	Description	Page
Activity Network Diagram/ Gantt Chart	Helps you keep track of your implementation plans.	27
Brainstorming	Enables your team to creatively and efficiently generate a large number of possible solutions.	45

Continued on the next page

Tool	Description	Page
Commitment Scale	Helps your team understand how much work must be done to achieve desired levels of commitment.	67
Control Charts	In the Improve step, these charts are used to show past and present performance of an indicator. Since Control Charts (and Run Charts) show plots of results as time passes, they are excellent tools for determining whether a solution has any real, lasting effect on your process.	75
Failure Mode and Effects Analysis (FMEA)	Used to anticipate potential problems, allowing your team to take counter-measures to reduce or eliminate risks.	111
Histograms	Comparing "before" and "after" Histograms shows how much progress has been made.	129
Involvement Matrix	Helps your team think about who should be involved in the different steps needed to make change a reality, as well as the level of involvement that is appropriate for each of them.	156
Pareto Chart	As with Histograms, comparing "before" and "after" Pareto Charts is a way to objectively see how much progress has been made.	178
PDCA Cycle/ Pilot	The PDCA (Plan-Do-Check-Act) Cycle is the basic methodology behind a pilot. A pilot is a test of the whole system on a small scale to evaluate a solution and to make its full-scale implementation more effective.	199
Prioritization Matrix	Helps you objectively evaluate alternative solutions to a problem. The key is reaching consensus on the relative importance of different criteria first and then weighting the alternatives against those criteria.	189

Continued on the next page

Tool	Description	Page
Process Sigma	The true gauge of the effectiveness of any solution will show up in the new process-sigma level.	204
Run Chart	Like a Control Chart, a Run Chart shows whether a solution has any real, lasting effect on your process.	221
Tollgate Review	A formal review process that helps keep the project on track and helps promote successful results.	247

The Control Step

Goals and outputs

The goal of the Control step is to maintain the gains you have made by standardizing your work methods or processes, anticipating future improvements, and preserving the lessons you learn from this effort.

The outputs of the Control step include the following:

- Documentation of the new method.
- Training of fellow employees in the new method.
- A system for monitoring the consistent use of the new method and for checking the results.
- Completed documentation and communication of the results, learnings, and recommendations.

Approach

The "Control Step" Process Flow

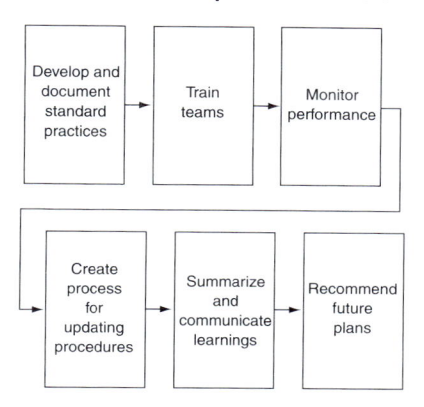

```
Develop and document standard practices → Train teams → Monitor performance → Create process for updating procedures → Summarize and communicate learnings → Recommend future plans
```

Many tools can help you monitor and control processes. Simply thinking in terms of PDCA (Plan-Do-Check-Act)—or, in this case, SDCA (Standardize-Do-Check-Act)—creates a mentality of constantly checking the effectiveness of your current methods. Training ensures consistency of application, as do "conspicuous standards" that make it easy for employees to do the job correctly.

The applicable tools for the Control step include the following:

Tool	Description	Page
Communication Plan	Helps you communicate effectively with the rest of the organization about the project.	70
Control Charts	Monitor progress over time after your project is completed. They can help your team continually quantify the capability of your process and identify when special events interrupt normal operations. It is typically part of the Process Management Chart.	75
PDCA Cycle	Serves as a reminder to think of improvement as being continual: Where can you go next to make the process even better?	199
Process Management Chart	Documents your PDCA—the plan for doing the work, how to check the results, and how to act if something undesirable or unexpected shows up. It also serves as a self-audit tool for checking how well and how consistently the new standards are applied.	199
Run Chart	Monitors progress over time after a project is completed. It is typically part of the Process Management Chart.	221
Six Sigma Storyboard	A pictorial record of your project. Typical documents include a succinct final report and a completed Storyboard that captures the project in graphical form.	239
Tollgate Review	A formal review process that helps keep the project on track and helps promote successful results.	247

DMAIC team structure

In most Six Sigma efforts, companies divide the responsibilities for accomplishing the improvement into four major roles: the sponsor; the team coach, typically called the Master Six Sigma Expert; the team leader, typically called the Six Sigma Expert; and the team member.

The DMAIC Team Structure

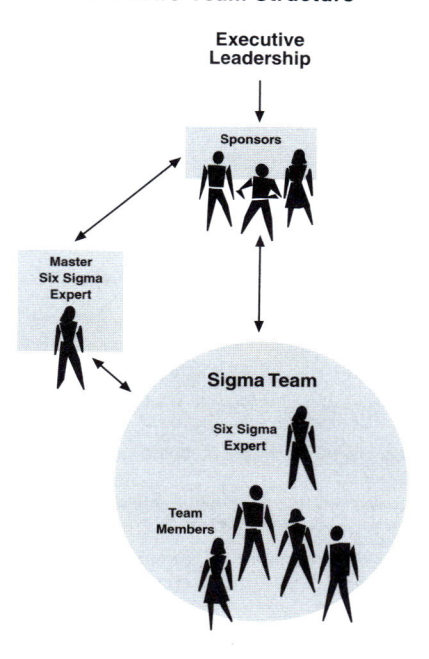

Early on in a Six Sigma project, it's important to clarify your team's relationship with your sponsor(s)—the supervisors, managers, or executives who have the power to allocate resources to the project, provide guidance regarding priorities, and ensure the project fits into your organization's business needs. Ongoing support and review by management are critical for your project's success, so part of the project plan should include activities such as weekly communication between the team leader and sponsors, as well as periodic reviews with the entire team.

You will likely also need technical support from a coach—an expert in Six Sigma improvement who has applied the many tools and concepts in practice. Such a person is often called a Master Six Sigma Expert by companies with a Six Sigma program. An organization typically has a few Master Six Sigma Experts who are called on by all its improvement teams.

The Six Sigma Expert leads the improvement team, managing all aspects of the project to meet the goals of the charter. The Six Sigma Expert typically has a strong knowledge of the tools and concepts, as well as some experience in applying them. The Six Sigma Expert might lead one or more teams at any given time, and in many organizations this is a full-time role.

Some organizations assign an additional team leader role, which is separate from the Six Sigma Expert role. In these cases, the Six Sigma Expert focuses on specific and more technical Six Sigma concepts, while the other team leader handles the responsibilities of team meetings, managing the project plan, and other less technical issues.

The team members carry out the work of the project. They learn many Six Sigma tools and concepts and apply these throughout the duration of the project. This book is designed to help you, the team member, make a successful contribution to your Six Sigma improvement team.

Activity Network Diagram (AND)
Scheduling sequential & simultaneous tasks

Why use it?

To allow a team to find both the most efficient path and realistic schedule for the completion of any project by graphically showing total completion time, the necessary sequence of tasks, those tasks that can be done simultaneously, and the critical tasks to monitor.

What does it do?

- All team members have a chance to give a realistic picture of what their piece of the plan requires, based on real experience
- Everyone sees why he or she is critical to the overall success of the project
- Unrealistic implementation timetables are discovered and adjusted in the planning stage
- The entire team can think creatively about how to shorten tasks that are bottlenecks
- The entire team can focus its attention and scarce resources on the truly critical tasks

How do I do it?

1. **Assemble the right team of people with firsthand knowledge of the subtasks**

2. **Brainstorm or document all the tasks needed to complete a project. Record on Post-it® Notes**

3. **Find the first task that must be done, and place the card on the extreme left of a large work surface**

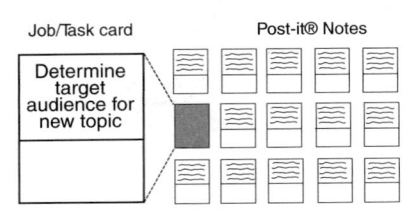

    Job/Task card   Post-it® Notes

    | Determine target audience for new topic |

4. **Ask: "Are there any tasks that can be done simultaneously with task #1?"**

    - If there are simultaneous tasks, place the task card above or below task #1. If not, go to the next step.

5. **Ask, "What is the next task that must be done? Can others be done simultaneously?"**

    - Repeat this questioning process until all the recorded tasks are placed in sequence and in parallel.

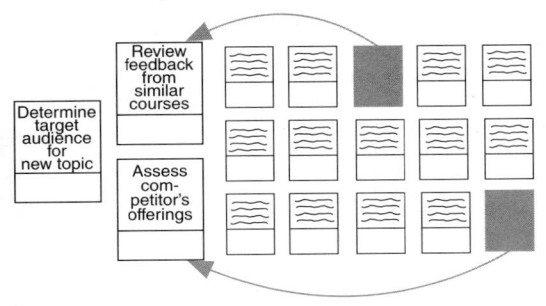

    | Review feedback from similar courses |
    | Determine target audience for new topic |
    | Assess competitor's offerings |

    Tip At each step always ask, "Have we forgotten any other needed tasks that could be done simultaneously?"

6. **Number each task, draw the connecting arrows, and agree on a realistic time for the completion of each task**

    • Record the completion time on the bottom half of each card.

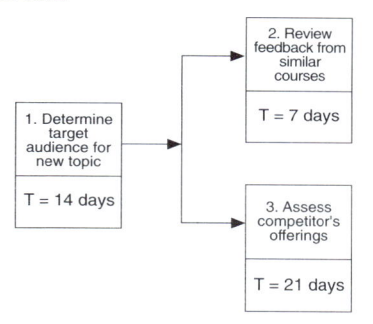

    ```
    ┌─────────────────┐      ┌─────────────────┐
    │ 1. Determine    │─────▶│ 2. Review       │
    │ target          │      │ feedback from   │
    │ audience for    │      │ similar         │
    │ new topic       │      │ courses         │
    │                 │      │                 │
    │ T = 14 days     │      │ T = 7 days      │
    └─────────────────┘      └─────────────────┘
             │
             │               ┌─────────────────┐
             └──────────────▶│ 3. Assess       │
                             │ competitor's    │
                             │ offerings       │
                             │                 │
                             │ T = 21 days     │
                             └─────────────────┘
    ```

    Tip Be sure to agree on the standard time unit for each task, e.g., days, weeks. Elapsed time is easier than "dedicated" time, e.g., 8 hours of dedicated time versus 8 hours over a two-week period (elapsed time).

7. **Determine the project's critical path**

    • Any delay to a task on the *critical path* will be added to the project's completion time, unless another task is accelerated or eliminated. Likewise, the project's completion time can be reduced by accelerating any task on the critical path.

    • There are two options for calculating the total critical path and the tasks included within it.

    Longest cumulative path. Identify total project completion time. Add up each path of connected activities. The longest cumulative path is the quickest possible implementation time. This is the project's *critical path*.

Calculated slack. Calculate the "slack" in the starting and completion times of each task. This identifies which tasks must be completed exactly as scheduled (on the *critical path*) and those that have some latitude.

Finding the critical path by calculating the slack

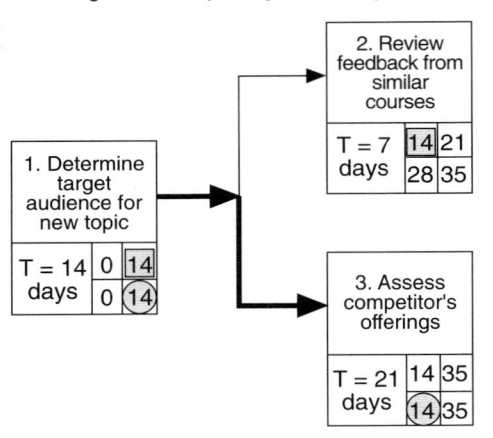

```
1. Determine target audience for new topic
T = 14 days | 0  | 14
            | 0  | (14)

2. Review feedback from similar courses
T = 7 days | 14 | 21
           | 28 | 35

3. Assess competitor's offerings
T = 21 days | 14 | 35
            | (14) | 35
```

Earliest Start (ES)	Earliest Finish (EF)
Latest Start (LS)	Latest Finish (LF)

ES = The *largest* EF of any *previous* connected task
EF = ES + the time to complete that task
LS = LF - the time to complete that task
LF = The *smallest* LS of any connected *following* task

When ES = LS AND EF = LF, that task is on the critical path, and therefore there is no schedule flexibility in this task.

Tip Determining the longest cumulative path is simpler than calculating the slack, but can quickly become confusing in larger ANDs.

The calculated slack option determines the total project and slack times; and therefore the total project time and critical path are identified "automatically."

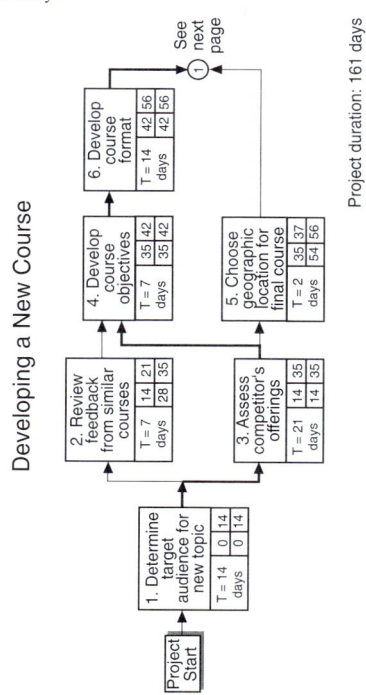

Developing a New Course

Project duration: 161 days

1. Determine target audience for new topic
T = 14 days | 0 | 14
        | 0 | 14

2. Review feedback from similar courses
T = 7 days | 14 | 21
          | 28 | 35

3. Assess competitor's offerings
T = 21 days | 14 | 35
           | 14 | 35

4. Develop course objectives
T = 7 days | 35 | 42
          | 35 | 42

5. Choose geographic location for final course
T = 2 days | 35 | 37
          | 54 | 56

6. Develop course format
T = 14 days | 42 | 56
           | 42 | 56

See next page →

Developing a New Course

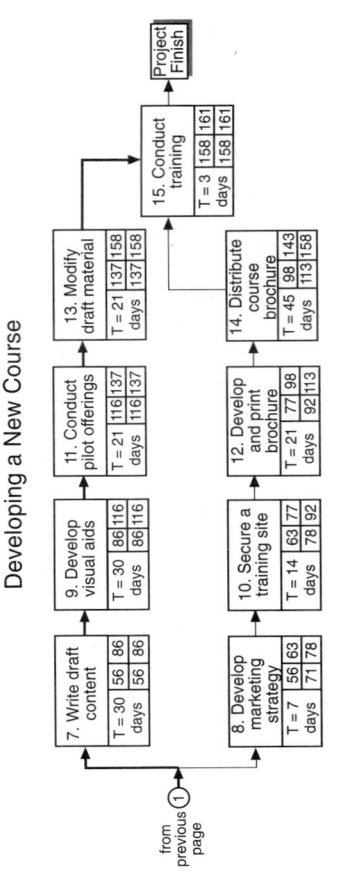

Variations

The constructed example shown in this section is in the Activity on Node (AON) format. For more information on other formats such as Activity on Arrow (AOA) and Precedence Diagram (PDM), see *The Memory Jogger Plus+®*.

Another widely used, schedule-monitoring method is the Gantt chart. It is a simple tool that uses horizontal bars to show which tasks can be done simultaneously over the life of the project.

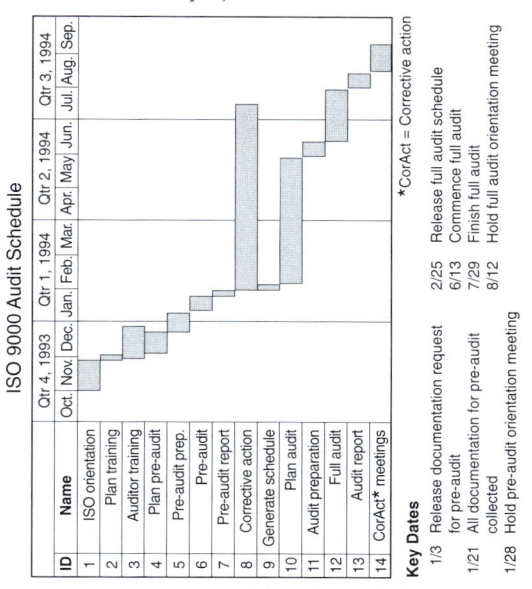

ISO 9000 Audit Schedule

ID	Name	Qtr 4, 1993 Oct. Nov. Dec.	Qtr 1, 1994 Jan. Feb. Mar.	Qtr 2, 1994 Apr. May Jun.	Qtr 3, 1994 Jul. Aug. Sep.
1	ISO orientation				
2	Plan training				
3	Auditor training				
4	Plan pre-audit				
5	Pre-audit prep.				
6	Pre-audit				
7	Pre-audit report				
8	Corrective action				
9	Generate schedule				
10	Plan audit				
11	Audit preparation				
12	Full audit				
13	Audit report				
14	CorAct* meetings				

*CorAct = Corrective action

Key Dates

1/3	Release documentation request for pre-audit
1/21	All documentation for pre-audit collected
1/28	Hold pre-audit orientation meeting
2/25	Release full audit schedule
6/13	Commence full audit
7/29	Finish full audit
8/12	Hold full audit orientation meeting

Information provided courtesy of BGP

Activity Network

Phase I
ISO 9000 Certification Audit Schedule

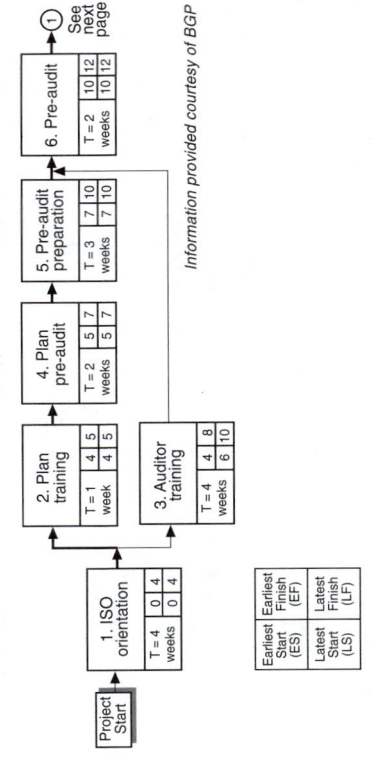

Information provided courtesy of BGP

```
Project Start
   ↓
1. ISO orientation
   T = 4 weeks
   ES: 0  EF: 4
   LS: 0  LF: 4
   ↓
2. Plan training          3. Auditor training
   T = 1 week                T = 4 weeks
   ES: 4  EF: 5              ES: 4  EF: 8
   LS: 4  LF: 5              LS: 6  LF: 10
   ↓
4. Plan pre-audit
   T = 2 weeks
   ES: 5  EF: 7
   LS: 5  LF: 7
   ↓
5. Pre-audit preparation
   T = 3 weeks
   ES: 7  EF: 10
   LS: 7  LF: 10
   ↓
6. Pre-audit
   T = 2 weeks
   ES: 10  EF: 12
   LS: 10  LF: 12
   ↓
  (1) See next page
```

Legend:
- ES = Earliest Start
- EF = Earliest Finish
- LS = Latest Start
- LF = Latest Finish

Activity Network

Phase I
ISO 9000 Certification Audit Schedule (cont.)

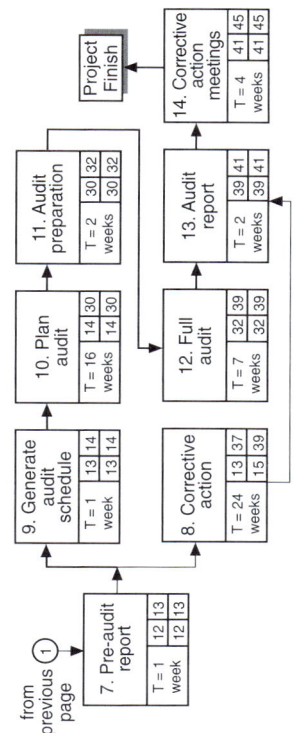

```
from          7. Pre-audit       9. Generate        10. Plan         11. Audit
previous 1 →  report         →   audit schedule →   audit        →   preparation    →  Project Finish
              T=1   12|13        T=1    13|14       T=16   14|30      T=2    30|32
              week  12|13        week   13|14       weeks  14|30      weeks  30|32

                                 8. Corrective      12. Full         13. Audit          14. Corrective
                                 action         →   audit        →   report         →   action meetings
                                 T=24   13|37       T=7    32|39     T=2    39|41       T=4    41|45
                                 weeks  15|39       weeks  32|39     weeks  39|41       weeks  41|45
```

Information provided courtesy of BGP

Note: The AND shows that the certification process will take 45 weeks. The bold arrow, indicating the critical path, clearly shows those tasks that must be completed as scheduled. The tasks off the critical path will also require careful monitoring since there is only two weeks of slack time in the schedule.

©2002 GOAL/QPC   Activity Network/Gantt 35

Planning Grid

A planning grid helps you identify the resources for, and outcomes of, each step in a project. The following features make it easy to use:

- Its table form quickly summarizes the tasks needed to complete a project.
- You can easily customize it to track information specific to your project.
- It is easy to create with pen and paper.

A Sample Planning Grid

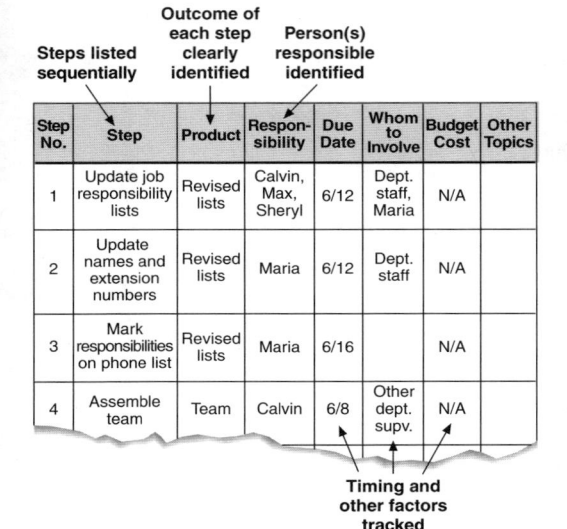

Steps listed sequentially — *Outcome of each step clearly identified* — *Person(s) responsible identified*

Step No.	Step	Product	Responsibility	Due Date	Whom to Involve	Budget Cost	Other Topics
1	Update job responsibility lists	Revised lists	Calvin, Max, Sheryl	6/12	Dept. staff, Maria	N/A	
2	Update names and extension numbers	Revised lists	Maria	6/12	Dept. staff	N/A	
3	Mark responsibilities on phone list	Revised lists	Maria	6/16		N/A	
4	Assemble team	Team	Calvin	6/8	Other dept. supv.	N/A	

Timing and other factors tracked

36 Activity Network/Gantt

The steps for completing a planning grid are as follows:

1. Specify the final outcome of the project.
2. Identify the final step and what it produces.
3. Identify the starting point and what it produces.
4. Brainstorm a list of steps that occur between the starting point and the final step.
5. Clean up the list by eliminating duplication, combining related ideas, rewriting unclear statements, and so forth.
6. Label the columns of a grid as shown in the example at left.
7. Write your final list of steps in sequence down the side of the grid.
8. Fill in the Product column for each step.
9. Enter a tentative due date or time for each step.
10. Revise steps if necessary.
11. Complete the remaining columns.

> ***Tip*** The categories across the top of the grid can vary, depending on the needs of your project.

Affinity Diagram
Gathering & grouping ideas

Why use it?
To allow a team to creatively generate a large number of ideas/issues and then organize and summarize natural groupings among them to understand the essence of a problem and breakthrough solutions.

What does it do?
- Encourages creativity by everyone on the team at all phases of the process
- Breaks down longstanding communication barriers
- Encourages non-traditional connections among ideas/issues
- Allows breakthroughs to emerge naturally, even on long-standing issues
- Encourages "ownership" of results that emerge because the team creates both the detailed input and general results
- Overcomes "team paralysis," which is brought on by an overwhelming array of options and lack of consensus

How do I do it?
1. **Phrase the issue under discussion in a full sentence**

> What are the issues involved in planning fun family vacations?

Tip From the start, reach consensus on the choice of words you will use. Neutral statements work well, but positive, negative, and solution-oriented questions also work.

2. **Brainstorm at least 20 ideas or issues**
   a) Follow guidelines for brainstorming.
   b) Record each idea on a Post-it® Note in bold, large print to make it visible 4–6 feet away. Use at minimum, a noun and a verb. Avoid using single words. Four to seven words work well.

   > What are the issues involved in planning fun family vacations?

   - Ask kids for ideas
   - Find a good range of price alternatives
   - Consider everyone's hobbies
   - Recall good vacations of the past
   - Use a creative travel agent
   - Combine vacation with business trip
   - Look at family pictures
   - Determine total budget
   - Find locations with activities for all ages

   Illustration Note: There are 10 to 40 more ideas in a typical Affinity Diagram

Tip A "typical" Affinity has 40–60 items; it is not unusual to have 100–200 ideas.

3. **Without talking: sort ideas simultaneously into 5–10 related groupings**
   a) Move Post-it® Notes where they fit best for you; don't ask, simply move any notes that you think belong in another grouping.

b) Sorting will slow down or stop when each person feels sufficiently comfortable with the groupings.

> What are the issues involved in planning fun family vacations?

- Ask kids for ideas
- Find a good range of price alternatives
- Use a creative travel agent
- Consider everyone's hobbies
- Combine vacation with business trip
- Find locations with activities for all ages
- Look at family pictures
- Determine total budget
- Recall good vacations of the past

Illustration Note: There are 5 to 10 more groupings of ideas in a typical Affinity Diagram

Tip Sort in silence to focus on the meaning behind and connections among all ideas, instead of emotions and "history" that often arise in discussions.

Tip As an idea is moved back and forth, try to see the logical connection that the other person is making. If this movement continues beyond a reasonable point, agree to create a duplicate Post-it®.

Tip It is okay for some notes to stand alone. These "loners" can be as important as others that fit into groupings naturally.

4. **For each grouping, create summary or header cards using consensus**

    a) Gain a quick team consensus on a word or phrase that captures the central idea/theme of each grouping; record it on a Post-it® Note and place it at the top of each grouping. These are *draft* header cards.

b) For each grouping, agree on a concise sentence that combines the grouping's central idea and what all of the specific Post-it® Notes add to that idea; record it and replace the draft version. This is a final header card.

c) Divide large groupings into subgroups as needed and create appropriate subheaders.

d) Draw the final Affinity Diagram connecting all finalized header cards with their groupings.

What are the issues involved in planning fun family vacations?

Define an ideal vacation through family consensus
- Ask kids for ideas
- Consider everyone's hobbies
- Look at family pictures

Determine the most your budget will buy
- Find a good range of price alternatives
- Combine vacation with business trip
- Determine total budget

Use multiple sources for vacation research
- Use a creative travel agent
- Find locations with activities for all ages
- Recall good vacations of the past

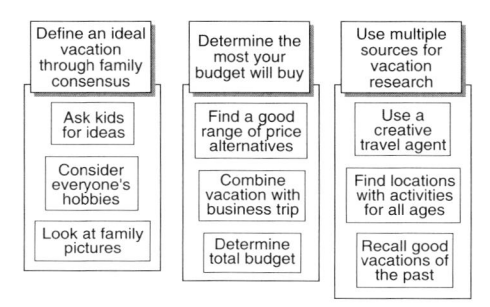

Illustration Note: There are 5 to 10 groupings of ideas in a typical Affinity. This is a partial Affinity.

Tip Spend the extra time needed to do solid header cards. Strive to capture the essence of *all* of the ideas in each grouping. ***Shortcuts here can greatly reduce the effectiveness of the final Affinity Diagram.***

It is possible that a note within a grouping could become a header card. However, don't choose the "closest one" because it's convenient. The hard work of creating new header cards often leads to breakthrough ideas.

Variations
Another popular form of this tool, called the KJ Method, was developed by the Japanese anthropologist Jiro Kawakita while he was doing fieldwork in the 1950s. The KJ Method, identified with Kawakita's initials, helped the anthropologist and his students gather and analyze data. The KJ Method differs from the Affinity Diagram described above in that the cards are fact-based and go through a highly structured refinement process before the final diagram is created.

Affinity

Issues Surrounding Implementation of the Business Plan

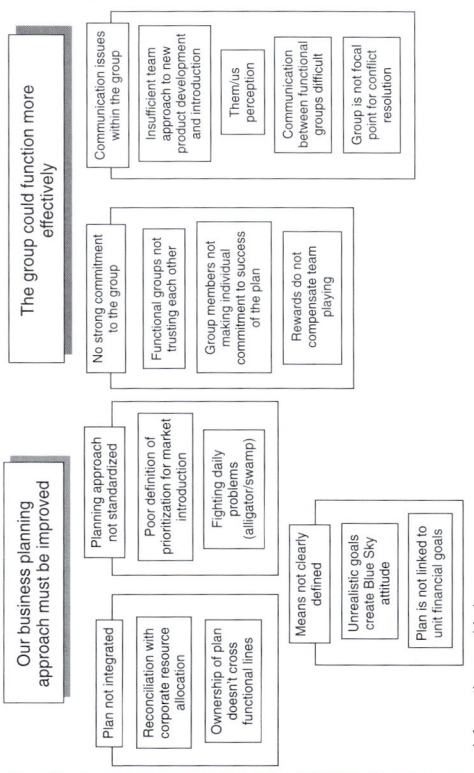

The group could function more effectively

- Communication issues within the group
  - Insufficient team approach to new product development and introduction
  - Them/us perception
  - Communication between functional groups difficult
  - Group is not focal point for conflict resolution

- No strong commitment to the group
  - Functional groups not trusting each other
  - Group members not making individual commitment to success of the plan
  - Rewards do not compensate team playing

Our business planning approach must be improved

- Planning approach not standardized
  - Poor definition of prioritization for market allocation
  - Fighting daily problems (alligator/swamp)

- Plan not integrated
  - Reconciliation with corporate resource allocation
  - Ownership of plan doesn't cross functional lines

- Means not clearly defined
  - Unrealistic goals create Blue Sky attitude
  - Plan is not linked to unit financial goals

More groupings on next page

Information provided courtesy of Goodyear

©2002 GOAL/QPC Affinity 43

Affinity

Issues Surrounding
Implementation of the Business Plan (cont.)

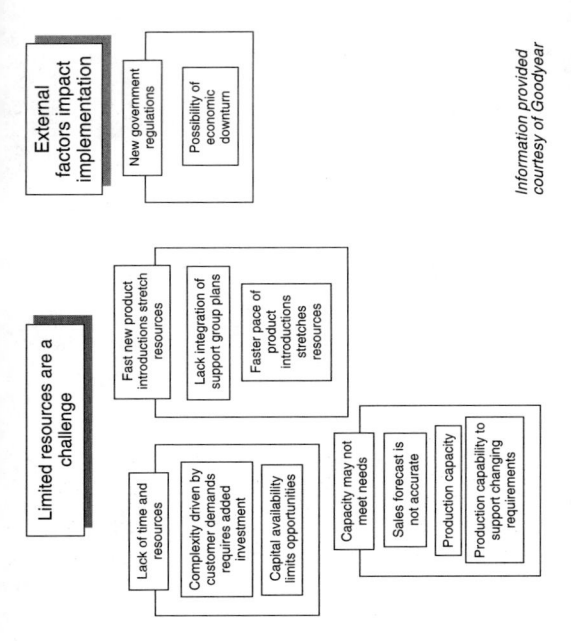

External factors impact implementation
- New government regulations
- Possibility of economic downturn

Limited resources are a challenge
- Fast new product introductions stretch resources
- Lack integration of support group plans
- Faster pace of product introductions stretches resources
- Lack of time and resources
- Complexity driven by customer demands requires added investment
- Capital availability limits opportunities
- Capacity may not meet needs
- Sales forecast is not accurate
- Production capacity
- Production capability to support changing requirements

Information provided courtesy of Goodyear

Note: The Affinity helped the team bring focus to the *many* opinions on business planning. The headers that surfaced became the key issues in the ID example (shown in the Interrelationship Digraph tool section).

44 Affinity ©2002 GOAL/QPC

Brainstorming
Creating bigger & better ideas

Why use it?

To establish a common method for a team to creatively and efficiently generate a high volume of ideas on any topic by creating a process that is free of criticism and judgment.

What does it do?

- Encourages open thinking when a team is stuck in "same old way" thinking
- Gets all team members involved and enthusiastic so that a few people don't dominate the whole group
- Allows team members to build on each other's creativity while staying focused on their joint mission

How do I do it?

There are two major methods for brainstorming.

- *Structured.* A process in which each team member gives ideas in turn.
- *Unstructured.* A process in which team members give ideas as they come to mind.

  Either method can be done silently or aloud.

Structured

1. **The central brainstorming question is stated, agreed on, and written down for everyone to see**

   Be sure that everyone understands the question, issue, or problem. Check this by asking one or two members to paraphrase it before recording it on a flipchart or board.

2. **Each team member, in turn, gives an idea. No idea is criticized. Ever!**

   With each rotation around the team, any member can pass at any time. While this rotation process encourages full participation, it may also heighten anxiety for inexperienced or shy team members.

3. **As ideas are generated, write each one in large, visible letters on a flipchart or other writing surface**

   Make sure every idea is recorded with the same words of the speaker; don't interpret or abbreviate. To ensure this, the person writing should always ask the speaker if the idea has been worded accurately.

4. **Ideas are generated in turn until each person passes, indicating that the ideas (or members) are exhausted**

   Keep the process moving and relatively short—5 to 20 minutes works well, depending on how complex the topic is.

5. **Review the written list of ideas for clarity and to discard any duplicates**

   Discard only ideas that are virtually identical. It is often important to preserve subtle differences that are revealed in slightly different wordings.

Unstructured

The process is the same as in the structured method except that ideas are given by everyone at any time. There is no need to "pass" since ideas are not solicited in rotation.

Variations

There are many ways to stimulate creative team thinking. The common theme among all of them is the stimulation of creativity by taking advantage of the combined brain power of a team. Here are three examples:

- **Visual brainstorming.** Individuals (or the team) produce a picture of how they see a situation or problem.
- **Analogies/free-word association.** Unusual connections are made by comparing the problem to seemingly unrelated objects, creatures, or words. For example: "If the problem was an animal, what kind would it be?"
- **6-3-5 method.** This powerful, silent method is proposed by Helmut Schlicksupp in his book *Creativity Workshop*. It is done as follows:

    a) Based on a single brainstorming issue, each person on the team (usually six people) has five minutes to write down three ideas on a sheet of paper.

    b) Each person then passes his or her sheet of paper to the next person, who has five more minutes to add three more ideas that build on the first three ideas.

c) This rotation is repeated as many times as there are team members, e.g., six team members = six rotations, six sheets of paper, eighteen ideas per sheet.

This interesting process forces team members to consciously build on each other's perspectives and input.

Cause & Effect/Fishbone Diagram
Find & cure causes, NOT symptoms

Why use it?

To allow a team to identify, explore, and graphically display, in increasing detail, all of the possible causes related to a problem or condition to discover its root cause(s).

What does it do?

- Enables a team to focus on the content of the problem, not on the history of the problem or differing personal interests of team members
- Creates a snapshot of the collective knowledge and consensus of a team around a problem. This builds support for the resulting solutions.
- Focuses the team on causes, not symptoms

How do I do it?

1. **Select the most appropriate cause & effect format. There are two major formats:**
   - **Dispersion Analysis Type** is constructed by placing individual causes within each "major" cause category and then asking of each individual cause "Why does this cause (dispersion) happen?" This question is repeated for the next level of detail until the team runs out of causes. The graphic examples shown in Step 3 of this tool section are based on this format.

- **Process Classification Type** uses the major steps of the process in place of the major cause categories. The root cause questioning process is the same as the Dispersion Analysis Type.

2. **Generate the causes needed to build a Cause & Effect Diagram. Choose one method:**
   - **Brainstorming** without previous preparation.
   - **Check Sheets** based on data collected by team members before the meeting.

3. **Construct the Cause & Effect/Fishbone Diagram**
   a) Place the problem statement in a box on the righthand side of the writing surface.
   - Allow plenty of space. Use a flipchart sheet, butcher paper, or a large white board. A paper surface is preferred since the final Cause & Effect Diagram can be moved.

Causes
"Bones"
(Major cause categories)

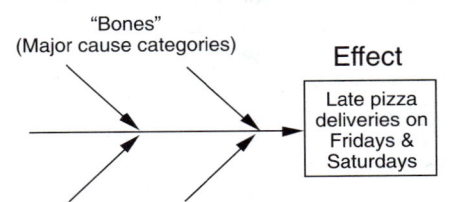

Effect
Late pizza deliveries on Fridays & Saturdays

Tip Make sure everyone agrees on the problem statement. Include as much information as possible on the "what," "where," "when," and "how much" of the problem. Use data to specify the problem.

b) Draw major cause categories or steps in the production or service process. Connect them to the "backbone" of the fishbone chart.

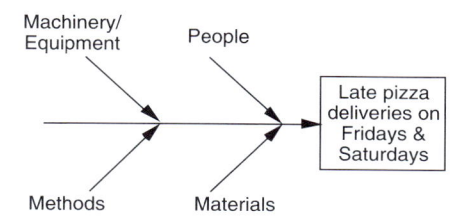

```
Machinery/
Equipment        People
        \         /
         \       /
          ↘    ↙
    ───────────────────→  ┌──────────────┐
          ↗    ↖          │ Late pizza   │
         /      \         │ deliveries on│
        /        \        │ Fridays &    │
   Methods    Materials   │ Saturdays    │
                          └──────────────┘
```

Illustration Note: In a Process Classification Type format, replace the major "bone" categories with: "Order Taking," "Preparation," "Cooking," and "Delivery."

- Be flexible in the major cause "bones" that are used. In a **Production Process** the traditional categories are: **Machines** (equipment), **Methods** (how work is done), **Materials** (components or raw materials), and **People** (the human element). In a **Service Process** the traditional methods are: **Policies** (higher-level decision rules), **Procedures** (steps in a task), **Plant** (equipment and space), and **People**. In both types of processes, **Environment** (buildings, logistics, and space) and **Measurement** (calibration and data collection) are also frequently used. *There is no perfect set or number of categories. Make them fit the problem.*

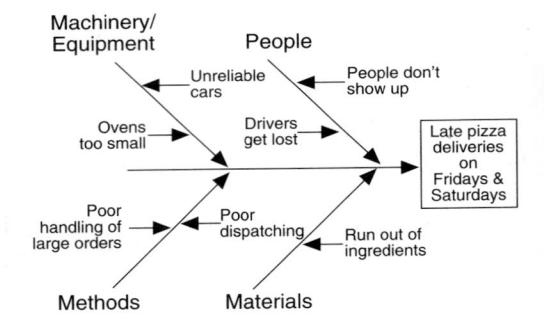

```
                                    People
Machinery/
Equipment         Unreliable    People don't
                    cars         show up
       Ovens       Drivers
     too small    get lost                    ┌──────────────┐
                                              │ Late pizza   │
─────────────────────────────────────────────▶│ deliveries   │
                                              │ on           │
       Poor                                   │ Fridays &    │
     handling of   Poor                       │ Saturdays    │
   large orders   dispatching  Run out of     └──────────────┘
                               ingredients
      Methods       Materials
```

c) Place the brainstormed or data-based causes in the appropriate category.

- In brainstorming, possible causes can be placed in a major cause category as each is generated, or only after the entire list has been created. Either works well but brainstorming the whole list first maintains the creative flow of ideas without being constrained by the major cause categories or where the ideas fit in each "bone."

- Some causes seem to fit in more than one category. Ideally each cause should be in only one category, but some of the "people" causes may legitimately belong in two places. Place them in both categories and see how they work out in the end.

Tip If ideas are slow in coming, use the major cause categories as catalysts, e.g., "What in 'materials' is causing . . . ?"

d) Ask repeatedly of each cause listed on the "bones," either:
- "Why does it happen?" For example, under "Run out of ingredients" this question would lead to

---

52 Cause & Effect/Fishbone

more basic causes such as "Inaccurate ordering," "Poor use of space," and so on.

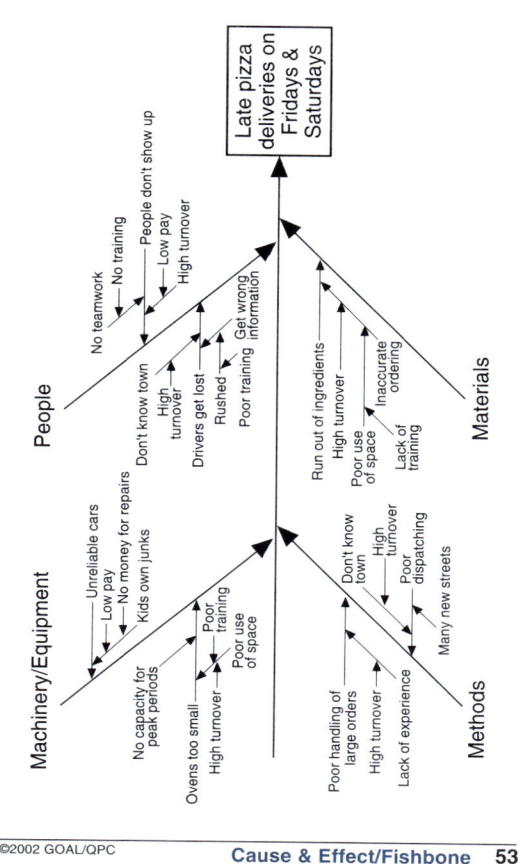

Late pizza deliveries on Fridays & Saturdays

People
- No teamwork
- No training
- People don't show up
- Low pay
- High turnover
- Don't know town
- High turnover
- Drivers get lost
- Rushed
- Poor training
- Get wrong information

Materials
- Run out of ingredients
- High turnover
- Poor use of space
- Inaccurate ordering
- Lack of training

Machinery/Equipment
- Unreliable cars
- Low pay
- No money for repairs
- Kids own junks
- No capacity for peak periods
- Ovens too small
- High turnover
- Poor training
- Poor use of space

Methods
- Poor handling of large orders
- High turnover
- Lack of experience
- Don't know town
- High turnover
- Poor dispatching
- Many new streets

Cause & Effect/Fishbone

- "What could happen?" For example, under "Run out of ingredients" this question would lead to a deeper understanding of the problem such as "Boxes," "Prepared dough," "Toppings," and so on.

Tip For each deeper cause, continue to push for deeper understanding, but know when to stop. A rule of thumb is to stop questioning when a cause is controlled by more than one level of management removed from the group. Otherwise, the process could become an exercise in frustration. Use common sense.

e) Interpret or test for root cause(s) by one or more of the following:
- Look for causes that appear repeatedly within or across major cause categories.

- Select through either an unstructured consensus process or one that is structured, such as Nominal Group Technique or Multivoting.

- Gather data through Check Sheets or other formats to determine the relative frequencies of the different causes.

Variations

Traditionally, Cause & Effect Diagrams have been created in a meeting setting. The completed "fishbone" is often reviewed by others and/or confirmed with data collection. A very effective alternative is CEDAC®, in which a large, highly visible, blank fishbone chart is displayed prominently in a work area. Everyone posts both potential causes and solutions on Post-it® Notes in each of the categories. Causes and solutions are reviewed, tested, and posted. This technique opens up the process to the knowledge and creativity of every person in the operation.

Cause & Effect/Fishbone
Bed Assignment Delay

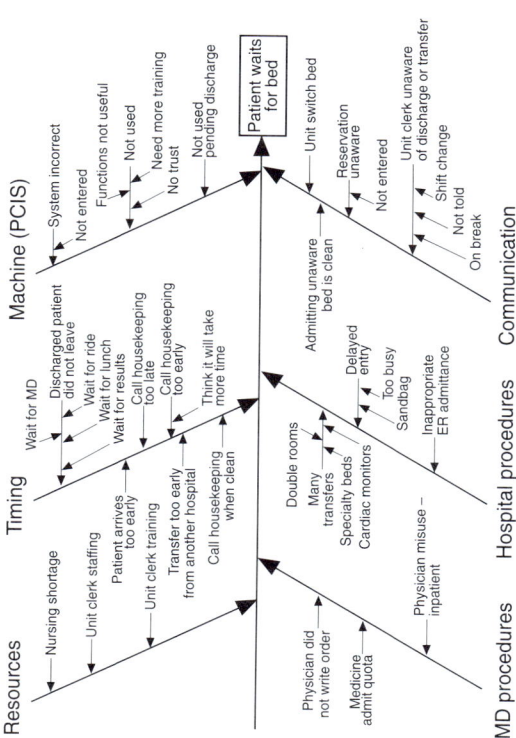

Effect: Patient waits for bed

Machine (PCIS)
- System incorrect — Not entered
- Functions not useful — Not used
- Need more training — No trust
- Not used pending discharge

Communication
- Unit switch bed
- Reservation unaware — Not entered
- Unit clerk unaware of discharge or transfer — Shift change — Not told — On break

Timing
- Wait for MD — Discharged patient did not leave
- Wait for ride — Wait for lunch
- Wait for results — Call housekeeping too late
- Call housekeeping too early
- Think it will take more time

Hospital procedures
- Admitting unaware bed is clean
- Delayed entry — Too busy
- Sandbag — Inappropriate ER admittance
- Double rooms
- Many transfers
- Specialty beds
- Cardiac monitors
- Physician misuse – inpatient

Resources
- Nursing shortage
- Unit clerk staffing
- Patient arrives too early
- Unit clerk training
- Transfer too early from another hospital
- Call housekeeping when clean

MD procedures
- Physician did not write order
- Medicine admit quota

Information provided courtesy of Rush-Presbyterian-St. Luke's Medical Center

©2002 GOAL/QPC

Cause & Effect/Fishbone

Causes for Bent Pins (Plug-In Side)

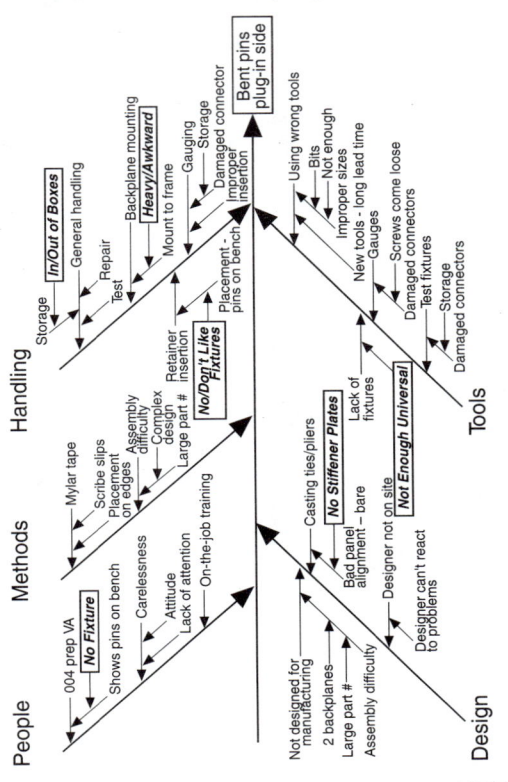

People
- 004 prep VA — *No Fixture*
- Shows pins on bench
- Attitude
- Lack of attention
- Carelessness
- On-the-job training

Methods
- Mylar tape
- Scribe slips
- Placement on edges
- Assembly difficulty
- Complex design
- Large part #
- Retainer insertion
- Placement - pins on bench
- *No/Don't Like Fixtures*

Handling
- Storage
- General handling
- Repair
- Test
- Backplane mounting
- Mount to frame
- Gauging
- Storage
- Damaged connector
- Improper insertion
- *In/Out of Boxes*
- *Heavy/Awkward*

→ **Bent pins plug-in side**

Tools
- Using wrong tools
- Bits
- Not enough
- Improper sizes
- New tools - long lead time
- Gauges
- Screws come loose
- Damaged connectors
- Test fixtures
- Storage
- Damaged connectors
- *Not Enough Universal*

Design
- Not designed for manufacturing
- 2 backplanes
- Large part #
- Assembly difficulty
- Designer can't react to problems
- Designer not on site
- Bad panel alignment – bare
- Lack of fixtures
- Casting ties/pliers
- *No Stiffener Plates*

Information provided courtesy of AT&T

Five Whys

This method helps you determine root causes quickly. Start with your focused problem and then ask "Why?" five times.

Example

Focused problem: Customers complain about waiting too long to get connected to staff when they call during lunch hours.

A Sample Implementation of the Five Whys Method

Sample focused problem: Customers complain about waiting too long to get connected to staff when they call during lunch hours.

The first three whys are progressively deeper, more specific, actionable causes. The problem-solving team should focus on the third why.

Why does this problem happen?
Backup operators take longer to connect callers.

Why does it take backup operators longer?
Backup operators don't know the job as well as the regular operators/receptionists do.

Why don't the backup operators know the job as well?
There is no special training or job aids to make up for the gap in experience, and they receive all their training on the job.

These broader causes are outside the scope of the problem-solving team and should be provided to management as data about systems issues that are deep causes of problems.

Why don't they have special training or job aids?
In the past, the organization has not recognized this need.

Why hasn't the organization recognized this need?
The organization has no system to identify training needs.

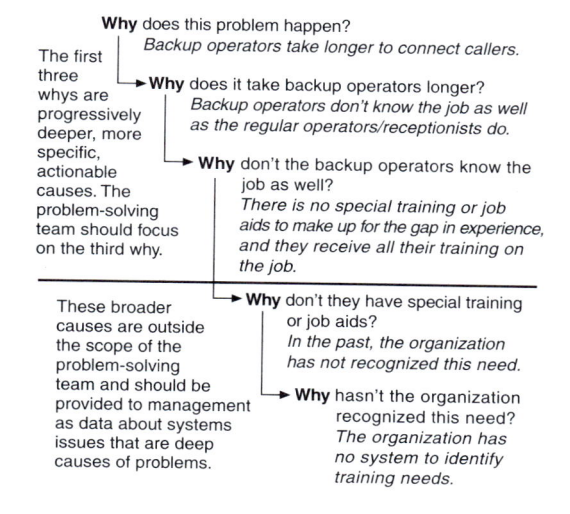

Tip As you probe down five or more levels, you might come up with different solution ideas that fit for each level. Where should you stop? What is the level at which you could take action?

- It depends on the scope of authority of the person or team investigating the problem.
- An immediate fix for the example on the previous page would be to provide at least some training for current backup operators.

As you push for deeper whys, record all of your ideas. You can then arrange them using another tool. This usually doesn't help directly with the problem you are addressing, but top management can use the data from a series of problems to address system and policy issues.

Charter
Framing the DMAIC project

Why use it?

To obtain an agreement between management and project team members about what the team will accomplish.

What does it do?

- Clarifies what is expected of the team
- Keeps the team focused
- Keeps the team aligned with organizational priorities
- Transfers ownership of the project from the leadership team and sponsor(s) to the project team

How do I do it?

Some charters are long and detailed; others are short and concise. All charters should include the elements listed below. Complete the six steps outlined below to create your charter. (See pages 13 through 17 of *The Project Management Memory Jogger™* for a sample charter. Another sample charter starts on page 63.)

1. **Develop an overview of the purpose of your project.**
   - The purpose describes the problem or opportunity your team is addressing.
   - The purpose answers the question "What is wrong?"

- Focus on what the team's goals are.
- The purpose should not include assumptions about causes of the problem or possible solutions.
- Additional questions to ask include the following:
  - What is important to customers about our product or service?
  - What problems do customers have with our product or service?
  - What problem is our team addressing?

2. **Develop one or more statements about why it is important to work on this project**
   - Describe the business case for the project:
     - Why is it important to customers?
     - Why is it important to our business?
     - Why is it important to employees?
     - Why should it be worked on now?
   - Estimate the project's potential impact on your business or the potential opportunity it can create.
     - Rough figures are OK.
   - Additional questions to ask include the following:
     - How will the reduction of defects impact our customers? The business? The employees?

   Tip Before they can fully commit to and support a project, the sponsors need to have at least a rough estimate of the project's business impact. They then have the opportunity to either buy into the project or suggest revisions in scope or direction that will improve the project's impact.

3. **Identify the *focus*, or *scope*, of the project. Scope does the following:**
    - Identifies the boundaries of the team's work: the start and end points of the process the team is improving, the stage at which project team members begin their work, and the stage at which their work ends.
    - Clarifies decision-making authority.
    - Clarifies budgetary limits.
    - Clarifies what is within the team's area of influence—as well as what is outside that area.
    - Includes the project's schedule and milestones.
    - Includes identifying checkpoints, or "tollgates," as reminders for the team to check with the sponsors at each major milestone.
    - Additional questions to ask include the following:
        – How will the team focus its work?
        – What information will you collect to identify urgent problems?
        – What specific parts of the process will you focus on?

4. **Determine the specific deliverables to be produced during the project**
    - The final deliverable goes to the customers of the project.
    - This deliverable can be a product, service, process, or plan.
    - A deliverable can be regarded as something that must be in place before changes can be accomplished.

- The types of deliverables for most projects are very similar. They include:
  - Process changes.
  - Training.
  - Documentation.
  - Other processes and procedures for maintaining gains.

5. **Define the measures or other indicators that will be used to (a) judge the success of the project and (b) identify ways to improve performance at a later date**
   - These measures/indicators do the following:
     - Establish a baseline of performance.
     - Are used to track progress.
     - Are used to judge the project's success.
   - If possible, identify the target and specifications for each measure.
   - Additional questions to ask include:
     - How much improvement is needed?
     - What defects will you be tracking?

6. **Determine the resources available to the team**
   - These resources consist primarily of the people who are available to join the team and do its work.
     - Include how much time they can spend on the project.
     - If they cannot be on the team, state the circumstances under which they can be involved with the project.
   - You can also include people who are not members of the team but might be called upon

by the team for additional information and expertise.

- Additional questions to ask include:
  - To whom is the team accountable?
  - Who is the team leader?
  - To whom can the team turn for expert guidance and coaching?
  - Has the process owner been identified?

Tip Every project needs a charter! If your sponsor has not provided it, then create one and get it approved.

Tip Write the charter in such a way that someone completely unfamiliar with the project could read it and understand what the project involves and why you are working on it.

Tip Most projects evolve; during each step, you learn more about what is really going on. Be open to revisiting the scope, definition, and purpose of your project. Check with your sponsor before making any substantive changes.

Sample Charter

Purpose

- Customers complain that it is frustrating to be unable to reach the appropriate party quickly when they call in. The Connect Time Team's purpose is to eliminate long waits for callers while they are being connected to their desired parties.

Importance

- *Customer Satisfaction*
  This is one of our four corporate strategic objectives.

How a phone call is handled is one of the first impressions a customer gets of our company. Surveys of customer satisfaction show "long wait time" as the #2 concern, second only to our pricing. Total elimination of this dissatisfier would increase overall satisfaction by 8 points. We assume a 50% improvement. Each point of satisfaction correlates with a revenue gain of $100,000 annually. $100,000 × 4 points = $400,000/year.

- *Revenue Increase*
  In addition to the revenue described above, we anticipate increased sales by having fewer potential customers drop off (i.e., hang up) while waiting for us to answer their calls. We average five hang-ups daily. Each caller orders an average of $400. We assume a 50% improvement. Five calls/day × $400/call × 250 days/year × 50% = $250,000/year.

Scope

- The team should focus its work on the process that takes place from the time a phone call comes in to the company until an appropriate person answers it. The team should consider ways to improve the operations of the current phone system—not investigate purchasing a new system.

- The team has authority to recommend solutions, including the purchase of new equipment, but it must get approval for all proposed solutions from its sponsors and the Operations Team. The office manager must approve any funding the team needs.

Measures
- A defect is considered to be a connection time of greater than thirty seconds.
- The team will be measured on its ability to reduce the time it takes to connect callers to a person who can help them with their questions. This will be tracked by following random calls through the process.

Deliverables
- The team should complete its work by February 15 and give a presentation to the Management Team.
- Develop and implement an improved process for connecting calls.
- Create a training program for the new process for all employees using existing communication channels.
- Provide a plan for ongoing monitoring and improvement of the process.

Resources
- *Team Sponsors*: Fred Smith, John Drucker
- *Team Members*: Ellen Hajduk, Customer Service Operator (Team Leader)
  Marjorie Andersen, Customer Service Operator
  Harry Cheng, Customer Service Operator
  Antonio Soto Diaz, Engineering
  Charmaine Jackson, Accounting
  Mary Scott, Information Services
  Mandy O'Neill, Sales and Service Supervisor
- *Coach*: Melissa Grant
- *Process Owner*: Kobe Oneal

- If the team decides it needs additional expertise, it must first check with the supervisor of the person with whom it wants to work.
- The team should not meet in excess of six hours per week without prior authorization from team members' supervisors.

Commitment Scale
Helping people commit to change

Why use it?
To identify and secure the support of, and remove the resistance of, people and systems vital to the accomplishment of the work.

What does it do?
- Identifies people or groups involved in or affected by a change
- Explicitly states the level of commitment required by each person or group before you can implement the change successfully
- Identifies the amount of work needed to bring people or groups to the level of commitment needed for you to implement the changes successfully
- Helps you set priorities and develop appropriate communication plans for different people or groups

A Sample Commitment Scale

Level of Commitment	People or Groups		
	Sales	Mgmt.	Cust.
Enthusiastic Will work hard to make it happen	●		●
Helpful Will lend appropriate support	↑	●	↑
Hesitant Holds some reservations; won't volunteer		↑	
Indifferent Won't help; won't hurt			X
Uncooperative Will have to be prodded		X	
Opposed Will openly state and act on opposition	X		
Hostile Will block at all costs			

How do I do it?

1. Identify the stakeholders involved in your project. Stakeholders are people who will be affected by the project or can influence it but are not directly involved with the project work.

2. List the stakeholder groups across the top of the commitment scale

3. Agree on the level of commitment needed by each stakeholder group for successful completion of the project. Indicate the level needed with a dot.

4. Agree on the current level of commitment of each stakeholder group. Indicate the current level with an X.

5. As a team, discuss the amount of change required to address any gaps between the current and required commitment levels

6. Develop a communication and action plan to address these gaps

The Components of a Commitment Scale

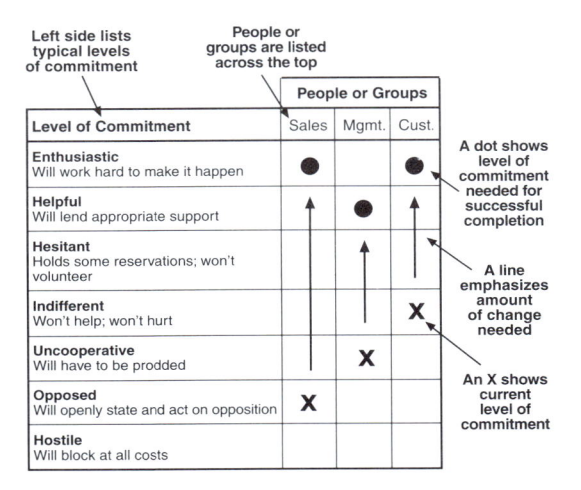

Left side lists typical levels of commitment

People or groups are listed across the top

Level of Commitment	Sales	Mgmt.	Cust.
Enthusiastic Will work hard to make it happen	●		●
Helpful Will lend appropriate support	↑	●	↑
Hesitant Holds some reservations; won't volunteer		↑	
Indifferent Won't help; won't hurt			X
Uncooperative Will have to be prodded		X	
Opposed Will openly state and act on opposition	X		
Hostile Will block at all costs			

A dot shows level of commitment needed for successful completion

A line emphasizes amount of change needed

An X shows current level of commitment

Communication Plan
Keeping people informed about the project

Why use it?
To plan how you will communicate with stakeholders for the duration of the project.

What does it do?
- Helps you identify and secure the support of, and remove the resistance of, people and systems vital to the accomplishment of the work
- Creates more buy-in
- Helps the team avoid pitfalls
- Identifies people or groups involved in or affected by a change
- Provides a vehicle for sharing the lessons learned from the project

How do I do it?

1. **During the Define step of the DMAIC method, identify the stakeholders involved in your project. Stakeholders are people who will be affected by the project or can influence it but are not directly involved with the project work.**

    - Typical stakeholders include the following:
        - Managers whose budgets, results, schedules, or resources will be affected by the project.
        - Process owners.
        - People who work on the process that you are studying.

- Internal departments or groups whose work feeds into the process or whose work depends on the process.
- Customers who purchase or use the output (i.e., the product or service) of the process.
- Suppliers who provide materials or services used by the process.
- Your organization's financial department.

2. **Identify the main concerns each group of stakeholders might have regarding the project**
3. **Develop a plan to give each group of stakeholders a report on the project's progress and to address their main concerns**

A Sample Communication Plan

Role	Who Names of people or groups	Main Concerns	Communication Notes When and how you will communicate with them
Team Leader (Six Sigma Expert) (If someone other than yourself)			
Team Member			
Sponsor(s)			
Team Coach (Master Six Sigma Expert)			
Process Owner			
Customers			
Other Stakeholders			

4. **Throughout the project, continue to regularly communicate with these stakeholder groups**

5. **Conduct "tollgate" reviews, which are formal reviews of the project's progress that are done at major milestones. Typically, tollgate reviews are conducted after each step in the DMAIC method.**

6. **When the team begins the Control step of the DMAIC method, plan for communication, closure, and recognition**

   • Summarize learnings.
     – About the work process:
       • What did you learn about the process that surprised you?
       • How much variation was in the process when your project began?
       • Are there other, similar processes in your organization?
     – About the team's process:
       • What did you learn about conducting a Six Sigma project?
       • What did you learn about working on a team? How well did team members work together?
       • What advice would you give to other teams?
       • How well did you work with your sponsor?
     – About your results:
       • Did you accomplish your mission? What factors helped your team? What factors hindered it?
       • What were your technical or business accomplishments?
       • Have the improvements been standardized and error-proofed? How will the improvements

be maintained? How were they communicated within and between work groups?

- What other discoveries did you make? How were they communicated within and between work groups?
- Have you used the PDCA Cycle on the changes you made?

Tip If time allows, or if there is a large volume of stakeholder concerns, you might want to use an Affinity Diagram to organize your team's list of ideas and brainstorm to decide what to do next. Then you can present the themes you identify to management and coworkers.

- Finalize documentation on improvements.
  - Finish your storyboard. It should contain your final results and conclusions.
  - Present the completed document to:
    - The sponsors.
    - The people whose jobs will change as a result of the work.
    - Customers affected by the change.
    - The stakeholders.
  - Collect and catalog the documentation and make it available to others.
- Summarize future plans and recommendations.
  - Have your team discuss the following issues and compile recommendations to submit to your sponsor or guidance team.
    - What are your recommendations for maintaining the gains already put in place? What role would you like your team to play?

- How much improvement is still needed to achieve your company's business goals?
- What parts of the problem still need to be addressed? Which are the most urgent?
- What would your team like to work on next, if approved by management? Where do you think management should devote company resources next?

• Communicate the results and future plans.
  – Communicating the team's results is a joint task for the project team and their sponsor.
  - If you haven't done so already, identify the people who will be involved in implementing the improved methods.
  - Which other employees could benefit from the lessons you learned?
  - How can you convey your team's results to management? To the rest of the organization?
  - How can the end of this project sow the seeds for future projects?

Tip When your team completes the Control step of the DMAIC method, you should be able to show your sponsor the following:

- Completed project documentation. Include a final storyboard that shows the results of your data analysis.
- Recommendations—supported by data, if possible—for next actions involving this process or ideas for a spin-off from this project.
- Plans for, or results from, communicating your achievements to the rest of the organization.
- Plans for celebrating your success.

Control Charts
Recognizing sources of variation

Why use it?

To monitor, control, and improve process performance over time by studying variation and its source.

What does it do?

- Focuses attention on detecting and monitoring process variation over time
- Distinguishes special from common causes of variation, as a guide to local or management action
- Serves as a tool for ongoing control of a process
- Helps improve a process to perform consistently and predictably for higher quality, lower cost, and higher effective capacity
- Provides a common language for discussing process performance

How do I do it?

There are many types of Control Charts. The Control Chart(s) that your team decides to use will be determined by the type of data you have. Use the Tree Diagram on the next page to determine which Control Chart(s) will best fit your situation. Other types of Control Charts, which are beyond the scope of this book, include the Pre-Control Chart, the Moving Average & Range Chart, and the Cumulative Sum Chart.

Based on the type of data and sample size you have, choose the appropriate Control Chart.

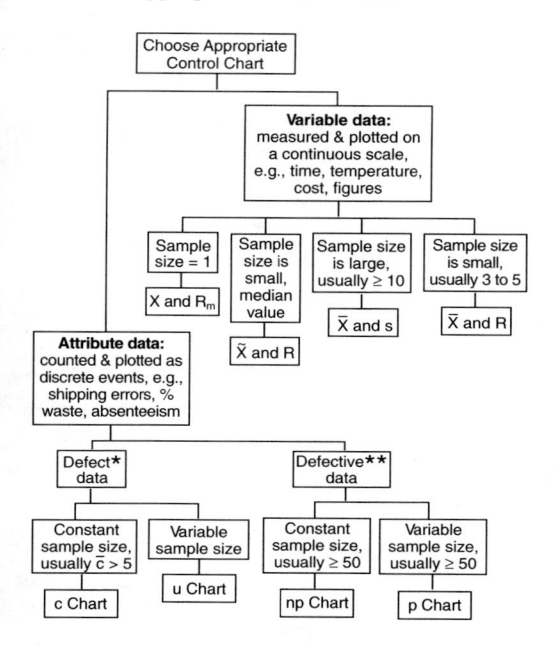

```
                    ┌──────────────────────┐
                    │ Choose Appropriate   │
                    │    Control Chart     │
                    └──────────────────────┘
                                │
                                ▼
                    ┌──────────────────────┐
                    │   Variable data:     │
                    │ measured & plotted on│
                    │  a continuous scale, │
                    │ e.g., time, temperature,│
                    │    cost, figures     │
                    └──────────────────────┘
```

Sample size is 1	Sample size is small, median value	Sample size is large, usually ≥ 10	Sample size is small, usually 3 to 5
X and R_m	$\tilde{X}$ and R	$\bar{X}$ and s	$\bar{X}$ and R

Attribute data: counted & plotted as discrete events, e.g., shipping errors, % waste, absenteeism

Defect* data

Constant sample size, usually $\bar{c} > 5$	Variable sample size
c Chart	u Chart

Defective** data

Constant sample size, usually ≥ 50	Variable sample size, usually ≥ 50
np Chart	p Chart

* Defect = Failure to meet one of the acceptance criteria. A defective unit might have multiple defects.

** Defective = An entire unit fails to meet acceptance criteria, regardless of the number of defects on the unit.

Constructing Control Charts

1. **Select the process to be charted**

2. **Determine sampling method and plan**
   - How large a sample can be drawn? Balance the time and cost to collect a sample with the amount of information you will gather. *See the Tree Diagram on the previous page for suggested sample sizes.*
   - As much as possible, obtain the samples under the same technical conditions: the same machine, operator, lot, and so on.
   - Frequency of sampling will depend on whether you are able to discern patterns in the data. Consider hourly, daily, shifts, monthly, annually, lots, and so on. Once the process is "in control," you might consider reducing the frequency with which you sample.
   - Generally, collect 20–25 groups of samples before calculating the statistics and control limits.
   - Consider using historical data to set a baseline.

   Tip Make sure samples are random. To establish the inherent variation of a process, allow the process to run untouched, i.e., according to standard procedures.

3. **Initiate data collection**
   - Run the process untouched, and gather sampled data.
   - Record data on an appropriate Control Chart sheet or other graph paper. Include any unusual events that occur.

4. Calculate the appropriate statistics

a) If you have attribute data, use the Attribute Data Table, Central Line column.

Attribute Data Table

Type Control Chart	Sample size	Central Line	Control Limits
Fraction defective p Chart	Variable, usually ≥50	For each subgroup: $p = np/n$ For all subgroups: $\bar{p} = \Sigma np/\Sigma n$	*$UCL_p = \bar{p} + 3\sqrt{\dfrac{\bar{p}(1-\bar{p})}{n}}$ *$LCL_p = \bar{p} - 3\sqrt{\dfrac{\bar{p}(1-\bar{p})}{n}}$
Number defective np Chart	Constant, usually ≥50	For each subgroup: np = # defective units For all subgroups: $n\bar{p} = \Sigma np/k$	$UCL_{np} = n\bar{p} + 3\sqrt{n\bar{p}(1-\bar{p})}$ $LCL_{np} = n\bar{p} - 3\sqrt{n\bar{p}(1-\bar{p})}$
Number of defects c Chart	Constant	For each subgroup: c = # defects For all subgroups: $\bar{c} = \Sigma c/k$	$UCL_c = \bar{c} + 3\sqrt{\bar{c}}$ $LCL_c = \bar{c} - 3\sqrt{\bar{c}}$
Number of defects per unit u Chart	Variable	For each subgroup: $u = c/n$ For all subgroups: $\bar{u} = \Sigma c/\Sigma n$	*$UCL_u = \bar{u} + 3\sqrt{\dfrac{\bar{u}}{n}}$ *$LCL_u = \bar{u} - 3\sqrt{\dfrac{\bar{u}}{n}}$

np = # defective units
c = # of defects
n = sample size within each subgroup
k = # of subgroups

* This formula creates changing control limits. To avoid this, use average sample sizes $\bar{n}$ for those samples that are within ±20% of the average sample size. Calculate individual limits for the samples exceeding ±20%.

b) If you have variable data, use the Variable Data Table, Central Line column.

Variable Data Table

Type Control Chart	Sample size n	Central Line*	Control Limits
Average & Range $\bar{X}$ and R	<10, but usually 3 to 5	$\bar{\bar{X}} = \dfrac{(\bar{X}_1 + \bar{X}_2 + \ldots \bar{X}_k)}{k}$	$UCL_{\bar{X}} = \bar{\bar{X}} + A_2\bar{R}$ $LCL_{\bar{X}} = \bar{\bar{X}} - A_2\bar{R}$
		$\bar{R} = \dfrac{(R_1 + R_2 + \ldots R_k)}{k}$	$UCL_R = D_4\bar{R}$ $LCL_R = D_3\bar{R}$
Average & Standard Deviation $\bar{X}$ and s	Usually ≥10	$\bar{\bar{X}} = \dfrac{(\bar{X}_1 + \bar{X}_2 + \ldots \bar{X}_k)}{k}$	$UCL_{\bar{X}} = \bar{\bar{X}} + A_3\bar{s}$ $LCL_{\bar{X}} = \bar{\bar{X}} - A_3\bar{s}$
		$\bar{s} = \dfrac{(s_1 + s_2 + \ldots s_k)}{k}$	$UCL_s = B_4\bar{s}$ $LCL_s = B_3\bar{s}$
Median & Range $\tilde{X}$ and R	<10, but usually 3 or 5	$\bar{\tilde{X}} = \dfrac{(\tilde{X}_1 + \tilde{X}_2 + \ldots \tilde{X}_k)}{k}$	$UCL_{\tilde{X}} = \bar{\tilde{X}} + \tilde{A}_2\bar{R}$ $LCL_{\tilde{X}} = \bar{\tilde{X}} - \tilde{A}_2\bar{R}$
		$\bar{R} = \dfrac{(R_1 + R_2 + \ldots R_k)}{k}$	$UCL_R = D_4\bar{R}$ $LCL_R = D_3\bar{R}$
Individuals & Moving Range X and R_m	1	$\bar{X} = \dfrac{(X_1 + X_2 + \ldots X_k)}{k}$	$UCL_X = \bar{X} + E_2\bar{R}_m$ $LCL_X = \bar{X} - E_2\bar{R}_m$
		$R_m = |(X_{i+1} - X_i)|$ $\bar{R}_m = \dfrac{(R_1 + R_2 + \ldots R_{k-1})}{k-1}$	$UCL_{Rm} = D_4\bar{R}_m$ $LCL_{Rm} = D_3\bar{R}_m$

k = # of subgroups, $\tilde{X}$ = median value within each subgroup

*$\bar{X} = \dfrac{\Sigma X_i}{n}$

5. Calculate the control limits

a) If you have attribute data, use the Attribute Data Table, Control Limits column.

b) If you have variable data, use the Variable Data Table, Control Limits column for the correct formula to use.

- Use the Table of Constants to match the numeric values to the constants in the formulas shown in the Control Limits column of the Variable Data Table. The values you will need to look up will depend on the type of Variable Control Chart you choose and on the size of the sample you have drawn.

Tip If the Lower Control Limit (LCL) of an Attribute Data Control Chart is a negative number, set the LCL to zero.

Tip The p and u formulas create changing control limits if the sample sizes vary subgroup to subgroup. To avoid this, use the average sample size, $\bar{n}$, for those samples that are within ±20% of the average sample size. Calculate individual limits for the samples exceeding ±20%.

6. Construct the Control Chart(s)

- For Attribute Data Control Charts, construct one chart, plotting each subgroup's proportion or number defective, number of defects, or defects per unit.
- For Variable Data Control Charts, construct two charts: on the top chart plot each subgroup's mean, median, or individuals, and on the bottom chart plot each subgroup's range or standard deviation.

Table of Constants

Sample size n	$\bar{X}$ and R Chart			$\bar{X}$ and s Chart			
	A₂	D₃	D₄	A₃	B₃	B₄	c₄*
2	1.880	0	3.267	2.659	0	3.267	.7979
3	1.023	0	2.574	1.954	0	2.568	.8862
4	0.729	0	2.282	1.628	0	2.266	.9213
5	0.577	0	2.114	1.427	0	2.089	.9400
6	0.483	0	2.004	1.287	0.030	1.970	.9515
7	0.419	0.076	1.924	1.182	0.118	1.882	.9594
8	0.373	0.136	1.864	1.099	0.185	1.815	.9650
9	0.337	0.184	1.816	1.032	0.239	1.761	.9693
10	0.308	0.223	1.777	0.975	0.284	1.716	.9727

Sample Size n	$\tilde{X}$ and R Chart			X and R_m Chart			
	Ã₂	D₃	D₄	E₂	D₃	D₄	d₂*
2	----	0	3.267	2.659	0	3.267	1.128
3	1.187	0	2.574	1.772	0	2.574	1.693
4	----	0	2.282	1.457	0	2.282	2.059
5	0.691	0	2.114	1.290	0	2.114	2.326
6	----	0	2.004	1.184	0	2.004	2.534
7	0.509	0.076	1.924	1.109	0.076	1.924	2.704
8	----	0.136	1.864	1.054	0.136	1.864	2.847
9	0.412	0.184	1.816	1.010	0.184	1.816	2.970
10	----	0.223	1.777	0.975	0.223	1.777	3.078

* Useful in estimating the process standard deviation $\hat{\sigma}$.

Note: The minimum sample size shown in this chart is 2 because variation in the form of a range can only be calculated in samples greater than 1. The X and R_m Chart creates these minimum samples by combining and then calculating the difference between sequential, individual measurements.

- Draw a solid horizontal line on each chart. This line corresponds to the process average.
- Draw dashed lines for the upper and lower control limits.

Interpreting Control Charts

- **Attribute Data Control Charts** are based on one chart. The charts for fraction or number defective, number of defects, or number of defects per unit measure variation *between samples*. **Variable Data Control Charts** are based on two charts: the one on top, for averages, medians, and individuals, measures variation *between subgroups* over time; the chart below, for ranges and standard deviations, measures variation *within subgroups* over time.

- Determine if the process mean (center line) is where it should be relative to your customer specification or your internal business objective. If not, then it is an indication that your process is not currently capable of meeting the objective.

- Analyze the data relative to the control limits, distinguishing between *common* causes and *special* causes. The fluctuation of the points within the limits results from variation inherent in the process. This variation results from common causes within the system, e.g., design, choice of machine, preventive maintenance, and can only be affected by changing that system. However, points outside of the limits or patterns within the limits come from a special cause, e.g., human errors, unplanned events, freak occurrences, that is not part of the way the process normally operates, or is present because of an unlikely combination of process steps. Special causes must be eliminated before the Control Chart can be used as a monitoring tool. Once this is done, the process will be "in control" and samples can be taken at regular intervals to make sure that the process doesn't fundamentally change. See "Determining if Your Process is Out of Control."

- Your process is in "statistical control" if the process is not being affected by special causes. All the points must fall within the control limits, and they must be randomly dispersed about the average line for an in-control system.

Tip "Control" doesn't necessarily mean that the product or service will meet your needs. It only means that the process is *consistent.* Don't confuse control limits with specification limits—specification limits are related to customer requirements, not process variation.

Tip Any points outside the control limits, once identified with a cause (or causes), should be removed and the calculations and charts redone. Points within the control limits, but showing indications of trends, shifts, or instability, are also special causes.

Tip When a Control Chart has been initiated and all special causes removed, continue to plot new data on a new chart, but DO NOT recalculate the control limits. As long as the process does not change, the limits should not be changed. Control limits should be recalculated only when a permanent, desired change has occurred in the process, and only using data *after* the change occurred.

Tip Nothing will change just because you charted it! You need to do something. Form a team to investigate. See "Common Questions for Investigating an Out-of-Control Process."

Determining if Your Process Is "Out of Control"

A process is said to be "out of control" if either one of these is true:

1. **One or more points fall outside of the control limits**

2. **When the Control Chart is divided into zones, as shown below, any of the following points are true:**

    ```
    - - - - - - - - - - -   Upper Control Limit
    _____Zone A_____      (UCL)
          Zone B
    _____Zone C_____
          Zone C            Average
    _____Zone B_____
          Zone A
    - - - - - - - - - - -   Lower Control Limit
                            (LCL)
    ```

   a) Two points, out of three consecutive points, are on the same side of the average in Zone A or beyond.
   b) Four points, out of five consecutive points, are on the same side of the average in Zone B or beyond.
   c) Nine consecutive points are on one side of the average.
   d) There are six consecutive points, increasing or decreasing.
   e) There are fourteen consecutive points that alternate up and down.
   f) There are fifteen consecutive points within Zone C (above and below the average).

Tests for Control

Source: Lloyd S. Nelson, Director of Statistical Methods, Nashua Corporation, New Hampshire

Common Questions for Investigating an Out-of-Control Process

- ☐ Yes ☐ No Are there differences in the measurement accuracy of instruments/methods used?
- ☐ Yes ☐ No Are there differences in the methods used by different personnel?
- ☐ Yes ☐ No Is the process affected by the environment, e.g., temperature, humidity?
- ☐ Yes ☐ No Has there been a significant change in the environment?
- ☐ Yes ☐ No Is the process affected by predictable conditions? Example: tool wear.
- ☐ Yes ☐ No Were any untrained personnel involved in the process at the time?
- ☐ Yes ☐ No Has there been a change in the source for input to the process? Example: raw materials, information.
- ☐ Yes ☐ No Is the process affected by employee fatigue?
- ☐ Yes ☐ No Has there been a change in policies or procedures? Example: maintenance procedures.
- ☐ Yes ☐ No Is the process adjusted frequently?
- ☐ Yes ☐ No Did the samples come from different parts of the process? Shifts? Individuals?
- ☐ Yes ☐ No Are employees afraid to report "bad news"?

A team should address each "Yes" answer as a potential source of a special cause.

Individuals & Moving Range Chart

IV Lines Connection Time

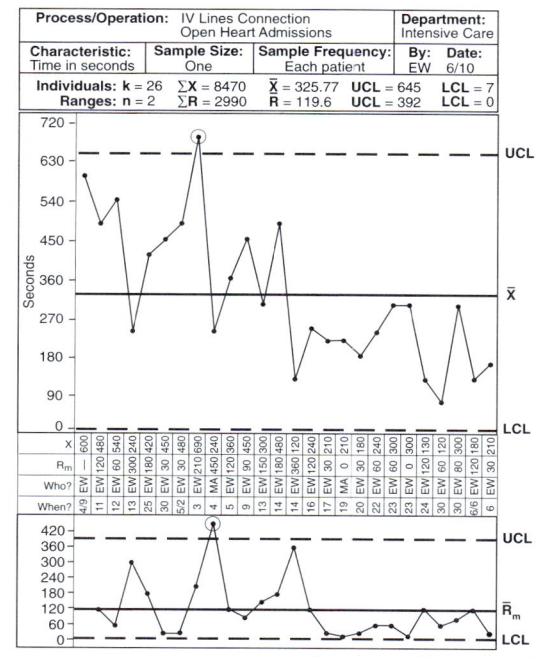

Process/Operation:	IV Lines Connection Open Heart Admissions		Department: Intensive Care	
Characteristic: Time in seconds	Sample Size: One	Sample Frequency: Each patient	By: EW	Date: 6/10
Individuals: k = 26 Ranges: n = 2	ΣX = 8470 ΣR = 2990	$\bar{X}$ = 325.77 $\bar{R}$ = 119.6	UCL = 645 UCL = 392	LCL = 7 LCL = 0

Information provided courtesy of Parkview Episcopal Medical Center

Note: Something in the process changed, and now it takes less time to make IV connections for patients being admitted for open heart surgery.

©2002 GOAL/QPC   **Control Charts** 87

p Chart
General Dentistry: Percent of Patients Who Failed to Keep Appointments

Historical Statistics:

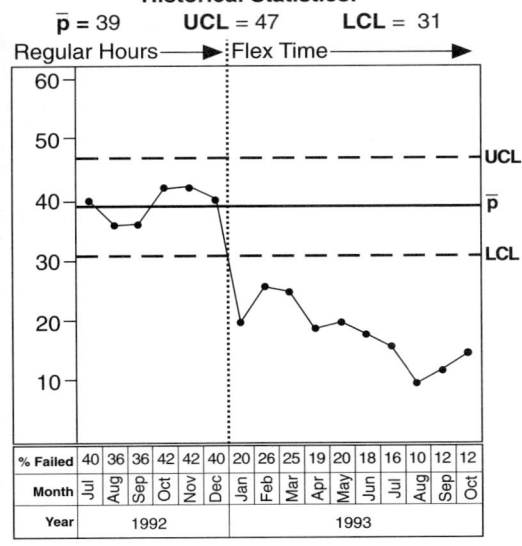

$\bar{p}$ = 39   **UCL** = 47   **LCL** = 31

Regular Hours ⟶ Flex Time ⟶

% Failed	40	36	36	42	42	40	20	26	25	19	20	18	16	10	12	12
Month	Jul	Aug	Sep	Oct	Nov	Dec	Jan	Feb	Mar	Apr	May	Jun	Jul	Aug	Sep	Oct
Year				1992							1993					

Information provided courtesy of U.S. Navy, Naval Dental Center, San Diego

Note: Providing flex time for patients resulted in fewer appointments missed.

u Chart

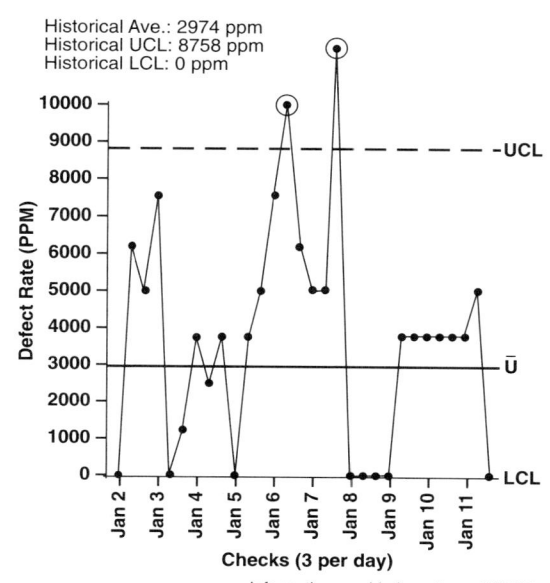

Shop Process Check
Solder Defects

Historical Ave.: 2974 ppm
Historical UCL: 8758 ppm
Historical LCL: 0 ppm

Information provided courtesy of AT&T

$\overline{X}$ & R Chart

n = 10 parts randomly sampled each hour

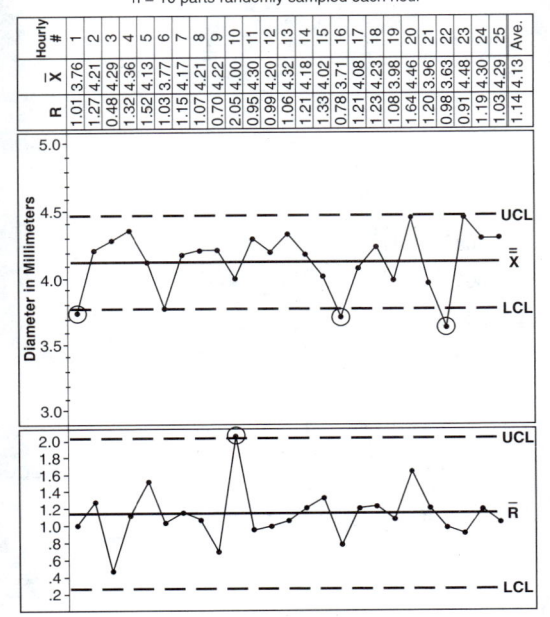

Hourly #	$\overline{X}$	R
1	3.76	1.01
2	4.21	1.27
3	4.29	0.48
4	4.36	1.32
5	4.13	1.52
6	3.77	1.03
7	4.17	1.15
8	4.21	1.07
9	4.22	0.70
10	4.00	2.05
11	4.30	0.95
12	4.20	0.99
13	4.32	1.06
14	4.18	1.21
15	4.02	1.33
16	3.71	0.78
17	4.08	1.21
18	4.23	1.23
19	3.98	1.08
20	4.46	1.64
21	3.96	1.20
22	3.63	0.98
23	4.48	0.91
24	4.30	1.19
25	4.29	1.03
Ave.	4.13	1.14

Information provided courtesy of BlueFire Partners, Inc., and Hamilton Standard

Note: Hours 1, 16, and 22 should be reviewed to understand why these sample averages are outside the control limits.

Critical To Quality (CTQ) Tree
Identifying measures from the customer's perspective

Why use it?

To identify Critical To Quality (CTQ) characteristics, features by which customers evaluate your product or service and that can be used as measures for your project. A useful CTQ characteristic has the following features:

- It is critical to the customer's perception of quality.
- It can be measured.
- A specification can be set to tell whether the CTQ characteristic has been achieved.

What does it do?

- Links customer needs gathered from your voice-of-the-customer (VOC) data-collection efforts with drivers and with specific, measurable characteristics
- Enables the project team to transform general data into specific data
- Makes the measuring process easier for the team

Setting Up a CTQ Tree

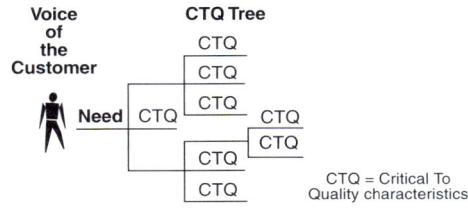

```
Voice              CTQ Tree
 of                  CTQ
the                  CTQ
Customer             CTQ
      Need   CTQ
                       CTQ
                       CTQ
                     CTQ
                     CTQ          CTQ = Critical To
                                  Quality characteristics
```

How do I do it?

1. **Gather sorted customer needs from your data-collection process.** The needs you use in the CTQ Tree can include the themes or specific needs from a Customer-Data Affinity Diagram (see below).

A Customer-Data Affinity Diagram

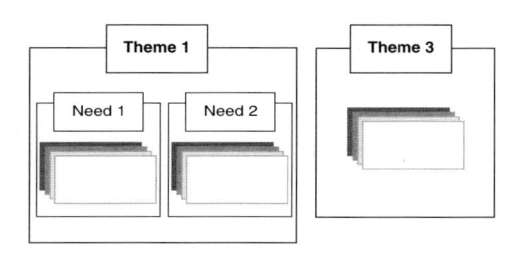

Tip Use the Kano Model (see page 158) prior to identifying CTQs to ensure your team has not missed any critical customer needs.

2. **List the major customer needs from the Customer-Data Affinity Diagram on the left side of the CTQ Tree**

3. **Try to view each need from the customer's point of view.** As you consider each need, ask, "What would that mean?" from the customer's standpoint. Each answer becomes a driver for the CTQs. Keep asking, "What would that mean?" until you reach a level where it would be absurd to continue. Your answers at this level are the CTQs.

Example:

- "Good customer service" means "knowledgeable reps."

- "Knowledgeable reps" means the answers they give are correct.
- It would be absurd to ask what "correct answers" means, so you should stop at this point. "Correct answers" is an appropriate CTQ.

A Sample CTQ Tree

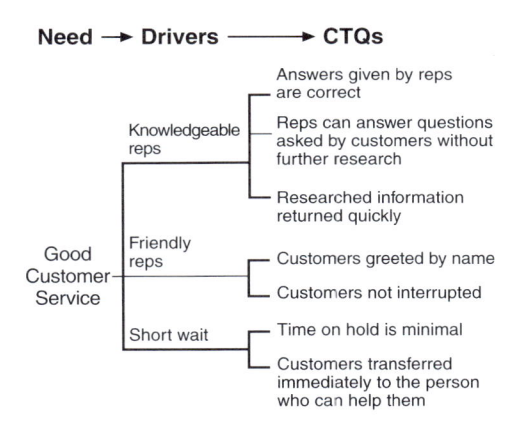

Need → Drivers ⎯⎯→ CTQs

Good Customer Service
- Knowledgeable reps
  - Answers given by reps are correct
  - Reps can answer questions asked by customers without further research
  - Researched information returned quickly
- Friendly reps
  - Customers greeted by name
  - Customers not interrupted
- Short wait
  - Time on hold is minimal
  - Customers transferred immediately to the person who can help them

General ←⎯⎯⎯→ Specific
Hard to measure ←⎯⎯⎯→ Easy to measure

4. **Select CTQs for the project based on the following:**
    - Which will have the greatest positive impact on the customer?
    - Which are within your scope or process area of focus?
    - Which of the Kano Model's "Must Be" characteristics are not addressed? (See the section on the Kano Model.)

5. **During the Define, Measure, and Analyze steps of the DMAIC method, the team will develop the process-output measures directly affecting the CTQs you select. These process-output measures are called y's. The team will also develop the causal factors directly affecting the y's, called the x's.**

    Tip In some cases you can go directly from the customer needs to the CTQs, while in others you might need to drive down through several levels of the CTQ Tree to discover the underlying CTQs.

Data Collection
Gathering meaningful data

Why use it?
To help you collect the right data for your needs and ensure the data you collect is useful and meaningful.

What does it do?
- Saves your team time and effort. You do preliminary thinking about what data will help you understand and explain when—and under what conditions—a problem does and does not appear.
- Structures your data collection so everyone understands what data will be collected and how
- Helps you think about how you can sort your data in a manner that might provide clues about a problem's causes

How do I do it?

Data-Collection Steps

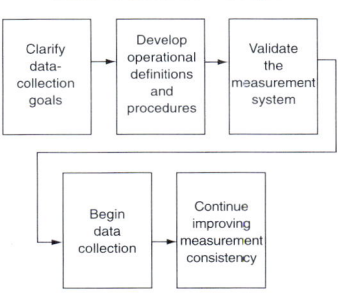

Clarify data-collection goals → Develop operational definitions and procedures → Validate the measurement system → Begin data collection → Continue improving measurement consistency

1. Clarify your data-collection goals

- Make sure the data you collect will give you the answers you need.
- Use the following questions to help you identify your data-collection goals.
  - Why are you collecting data? What questions do you want to answer?
  - What will you do with the data?
  - How will the data help you?
  - What patterns or relationships might you want to explore?
- Consider how you will stratify the data. *Stratification* means dividing data into groups, or strata, based on key characteristics.
  - A *key characteristic* is some aspect of the data that you think can help explain when, where, and/or why a problem exists.
  - The purpose of dividing data into groups is to detect a pattern that localizes a problem or explains why the problem's frequency or impact varies among different times, locations, or conditions.
- Typical stratification groups are based on the following:
  - Who—which people, groups, departments, or organizations are involved.
  - What—relevant machines, equipment, products, services, or supplies.
  - Where—the physical location of the defect or problem.
  - When—time of day, day of the week, or step of the process involved.

2. **Develop operational definitions and procedures. (See the section on Operational Definitions for details.)**

   Operational definitions tell you how you should measure something. They help you specify who should collect the data using what instrument, what data-collection form they should use, and whether they should measure each item or just a sample of the items.

   Sampling is useful when you don't need to collect data about every available occurrence to understand the process. Often you can learn much about a process from a relatively small amount of data. When sampling, take care to ensure that the sample represents all the data so that it gives an accurate, complete picture of the whole process. Your Six Sigma Expert should develop your sampling plan, which should specify what units to sample and how many samples to take.

3. **Validate the measurement system. (See the section on Measurement Systems Analysis for details.)**

4. **Begin data collection. This involves training the data collectors, piloting and error-proofing the data-collection process, and deciding how you will display your data.**

   Tip When the data-collection process begins, someone from the team who was involved in setting up the data-collection plan should be on hand to address any unanticipated issues that might arise.

5. **Continue improving your measurement consistency.** Check to make sure that everyone is following the data-collection procedures and that you make changes as necessary to adapt to changing conditions.

Tip Collecting data is a balancing act. You don't want your team to spend extra time collecting data because either you didn't get enough of it, or you didn't collect the right kind, in the first place. Conversely, you don't want to be buried in so much data that you cannot reasonably analyze or understand it given the time and methods available to you. Part of the challenge of data collection, therefore, is to decide just how much data will be sufficient and representative of the problem you wish to solve.

Tip If you already have experience with the DMAIC method and are familiar with the data tools, take time during this preliminary planning step to ensure you'll be able to analyze the data in ways that will answer your questions. Pretending you have the data in hand, make a sketch showing what an appropriate data plot looks like. Does it reveal the answers you need? For example, if you want to know if a problem is improving or worsening with time, you should use data that is collected in chronological order and suitable for plotting on Run Charts or Control Charts.

Tip For data collection involving voice-of-the-customer (VOC) data, see the section on VOC Data-Collection Systems and use the following VOC Data-Collection Plan Form.

Data-Collection Plan Form

**Data-Collection Plan
PROJECT:**

What questions do you want to answer?

Data		Operational Definition and Procedures			
What	Measure type/ data type	How measured[1]	Related conditions to record[2]	Sampling notes	How/where recorded (attach form)

How will you ensure consistency and stability?

What is your plan for starting data collection? (Attach details if necessary.)

Notes

[1] Include the unit of measurement where appropriate. Be sure to test and monitor any measurement procedures/instruments.

[2] Related conditions are stratification factors or potential causes you want to monitor as you collect data.

How will the data be displayed? (Sketch on additional sheet.)

©2002 GOAL/QPC   **Data Collection**   99

VOC Data-Collection Plan Form

VOC Data-Collection Plan
PROJECT:

Who	What and Why
Customers and Segments	Indicate specifically what you want to know about your customers. Develop customized versions of the following questions that you can ask during face-to-face interviews. • What's important to you? • What's a defect? • How are we doing? How do we compare to our competitors? • What do you like? What don't you like?

Sources

Put an X next to the data sources you think will be useful for this project.

Reactive Sources
- ❏ Complaints
- ❏ Problem or service hotlines
- ❏ Technical-support calls
- ❏ Customer-service calls
- ❏ Claims, credits
- ❏ Sales reporting
- ❏ Product-return information
- ❏ Warranty claims
- ❏ Web page activity
- ❏ Other:

Proactive Sources
- ❏ Interviews
- ❏ Focus groups
- ❏ Surveys
- ❏ Comment cards
- ❏ Sales visits/calls
- ❏ Direct observation
- ❏ Market research/monitoring
- ❏ Benchmarking
- ❏ Quality scorecards
- ❏ Other:

Summary: Which, How Many, How, and When

On a separate sheet, summarize your plans to gather and use reactive and proactive sources. Indicate how much data you will get, how you will get it, and when. Include, for instance, the number of interviews or surveys you plan to conduct, which customers you will contact, when you will start and end the data-collection process, and so on.

Data Points
Turning data into information

What type of data do you have?
- Words?
- Numbers?
  - *Attribute data?* Attribute data can be counted and plotted as discrete events. It includes the count of the numbers or percentages of good or bad, right or wrong, pass or fail, yes or no.

    Example: Number of correct answers on a test, number of mistakes per typed page, percent defective product per shift.

  - *Variable data?* Variable data can be measured and plotted on a continuous scale.

    Example: Length, time, volume, weight.

Do you need to collect data?
- If you need to know the performance of an entire population, the more economical and less time consuming method is to draw a sample from a population. With a sample, you can make inferences about, or predict, the performance of a population. Basic sampling methods are:
  - *Random.* Each and every observation or data measure has an equally likely chance of being selected. Use a random number table or random number generator to select the samples.
  - *Sequential.* Every *nth* sample is selected.
  - *Stratified.* A sample is taken from stratified data groups.

Can you categorize your data into subgroups?

- When you stratify data, you break it down into meaningful subcategories or classifications, and from this point you can focus your problem solving.

    Example: Data often comes from many sources but is treated as if coming from one. Data on minor injuries for a plant may be recorded as a single figure, but that number is actually the sum total of injuries by 1) type (cuts, burns, scrapes), 2) location (eyes, hands, feet), and 3) department (maintenance, shipping, production). Below is an example of how data has been stratified by plant department.

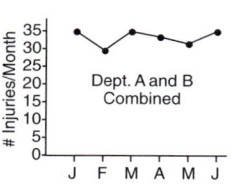

(Appears fairly stable over time.)

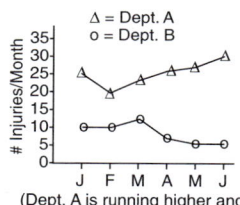

(Dept. A is running higher and may be increasing over time.)

What patterns are important in your data?

Predictable patterns or distributions can be described with statistics.

- **Measures of location**
    - *Mean* (or average). Represented by $\bar{X}$ (or X-bar), the mean is the sum of the values of the sample ($X_1, X_2, X_3 \ldots X_n$) divided by the total number (n) of sampled data.

    Example: For the sample: (3, 5, 4, 7, 5)
    $$\bar{X} = \frac{(3 + 5 + 4 + 7 + 5)}{5} = 4.8$$

– *Median.* When sampled data are rank ordered, lowest to highest, the median is the middle number.

Example: For the sample: (3, 5, 4, 7, 5)
Median of (3, 4, 5, 5, 7) = 5

When there are an even number of values, the median is the average of the middle two values.

Example: For the sample: (2, 5, 7, 4, 5, 3)
Median of (2, 3, 4, 5, 5, 7) = 4.5

– *Mode.* The most frequently occurring value(s) in a sample.

Example: For the sample: (3, 5, 4, 7, 5)
Mode = 5

- **Measures of variation**
  – *Range.* Represented by R, the range is the difference between the highest data value (X_{max}) and the lowest data value (X_{min}).

  Example: For the sample: (3, 5, 4, 7, 5)
  R = 7 – 3 = 4

  – *Standard Deviation.* Represented by s, the standard deviation of a sample measures the variation of the data around the mean. The less variation there is of the data values about the mean, $\overline{X}$, the closer s will be to zero (0).

Example: For the sample: (3, 5, 4, 7, 5) $\bar{X} = 4.8$

$$s = \sqrt{\frac{[(3-4.8)^2 + (5-4.8)^2 + (4-4.8)^2 + (7-4.8)^2 + (5-4.8)^2]}{5-1}}$$

$$= \sqrt{\frac{[3.24 + .04 + .64 + 4.84 + .04]}{4}}$$

$$= \sqrt{\frac{8.8}{4}}$$

$$= \sqrt{2.2}$$

$$= 1.48$$

The square of the standard deviation, *s*, is referred to as the *variance*. Variance is not discussed in this book.

Design of Experiments (DOE)
Testing multiple causes

Why use it?

With most data-analysis methods, you observe what happens in a process without intervening. With a designed experiment, you change the process settings to see the effect this has on the process output. The term *design of experiments* refers to the structured way you change these settings so that you can study the effects of changing multiple settings simultaneously.

This active approach allows you to effectively and efficiently explore the relationship between multiple process variables (x's) and the output, or process performance variables (y's). This tool is most commonly used in the Analyze step of the DMAIC method as an aid in identifying and quantifying the key drivers of variation, and in the Improve step as an aid in selecting the most effective solutions from a long list of possibilities.

What does it do?

- Identifies the "vital few" sources of variation (x's)—the factors that have the biggest impact on the results
- Identifies the x's that have little effect on the results
- Quantifies the effects of the important x's, including their interactions
- Produces an equation that quantifies the relationship between the x's and the y's
- Predicts how much gain or loss will result from changes in process conditions

How do I do it?

1. **Get background information on the problem**
    - Study available data from the Define, Measure, and Analyze steps of the DMAIC method.
    - Examine internal and external literature about solutions to the problem.
    - Clarify the experimental budget and constraints.

2. **Identify responses, factors, and factor levels**
    - Select one or more measurable responses (y's).
    - Define the measurement procedure for each y.
    - Identify all the factors (x's) that might impact each y.
    - Consider all pairs of factors that might interact (i.e., act quite differently in combination than they do alone).
    - Determine the high and low experimental levels for each factor.
    - Review combinations of factor levels for potential problems.

3. **Select the design**
    - Select a design appropriate for your current level of knowledge that allows you to examine the desired number of factors.
    - Decide on the number of experimental trials, or runs, you will perform.
    - If possible, build some replication into the final design; consider how large a defect must be for a customer to detect it.
    - Randomize the order of the runs whenever possible.
    - Consider the need for blocking. If you can conduct only a certain number of the experimental runs

under a similar set of conditions (e.g., only eight samples fit into an oven, so you must bake the other eight samples separately), then you need to run a blocked experiment. *Blocking* means determining which runs belong together under the same set of conditions. You must consider such blocking arrangements when you make your subsequent analysis.

4. **Collect the data**
   - Prepare a data-collection form that has room for all pertinent information, including written comments.
   - Schedule the needed equipment, people, and materials.
   - If necessary, provide training to everyone involved in doing the experiment, including those who will randomize and run the tests, take measurements, and so on.
   - Label and save all samples and results if possible.
   - Be present during the experiment process to monitor its performance carefully; keep a logbook of events, especially deviations from the plan.
   - Review the raw data as it is collected and correct any mistakes immediately.

5. **Analyze the data**
   - Plot the raw data in various ways.
   - If the experiment includes replications, compute averages, standard deviations, and residuals for each experimental condition and plot them in various ways.
   - Compute the factors' effects and interactions and plot them in various ways.
   - Where useful, develop a prediction model to relate factors to responses.

- When appropriate, confirm impressions from plots with appropriate statistical analysis.

6. **Draw, verify, and report your conclusions**
    - Interpret the results of the experiment using only known information (i.e., that which is theoretical or observed).
    - Formulate and write conclusions in simple, non-statistical language that others can understand.
    - Verify your conclusions with additional runs.
    - When appropriate, go on to the next iteration of your study.
    - Prepare a written report of the conclusions and recommendations to finish the Analyze step of the DMAIC method.

7. **Implement recommendations**
    - Continue with the Improve and Control steps of the DMAIC method.

    Tip Use a Cause & Effect Diagram as an integral part of your discussion to identify and select the factors (x's) to use.

    Tip The most difficult parts of this process are Step 3 (selecting the design), Step 4 (collecting the data), and Step 5 (analyzing the data). The team's Six Sigma Expert or Master Six Sigma Expert should lead these steps and explain them to the team when it is appropriate to do so.

    Tip Plan on using no more than 25% of your entire experimental budget on the first set of runs. Follow-up experiments are usually necessary to get additional information or to confirm what was already learned.

Variations

Many different experimental designs fall under the heading of "design of experiments." Listed below are some common design types used in Six Sigma improvement processes.

- Two-level fractional factorial screening designs: used to identify the vital few x's from many potential factors.
- Two-level full- and high-resolution fractional designs: used to help a team understand how the important factors act together to influence the response.
- Robust designs, or Taguchi designs: used to study the effect of the factors on not just the average response (y) but also on the amount of variation in the y.
- Response surface methodology: used to determine optimum settings for important factors.
- Evolutionary operation, or EVOP: used to experiment on a process while it is "on-line." If you limit the changes you make to the factor levels, all output produced might still meet customer requirements.

Sample Experiment

A team conducted an experiment to study the effects of three factors (script used, gender of caller, and age of caller) on an outbound telephone-sales process. They studied what the caller said during the call (Script A or B), whether the caller was male or female, and whether the caller had a young voice or an old voice (age = 20 or age = 60). All combinations of these factors are shown in the chart on the next page and are represented on the cube. The team then determined how many sales the callers made in a given time period (e.g., four hours of calling) and recorded the results in a table and plotted them on a cube by filling in the appropriate circle with the result (see below).

Results from the Sample Experiment

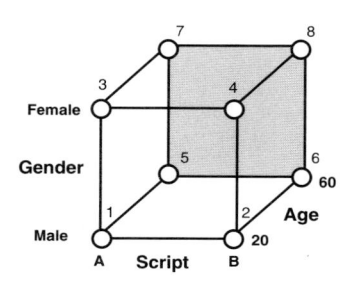

Standard Order	Script	Gender	Age	y = No. of Sales
1	A	Male	20	____
2	B	Male	20	____
3	A	Female	20	____
4	B	Female	20	____
5	A	Male	60	____
6	B	Male	60	____
7	A	Female	60	____
8	B	Female	60	____

110 Design of Experiments (DOE)

Failure Mode and Effects Analysis (FMEA)
Anticipating & preventing failures

Why use it?

Failure Mode and Effects Analysis (FMEA) is used to identify specific ways in which a product, process, or service might fail and to then develop countermeasures targeted at those specific failures. This will improve performance, quality, reliability, and safety. FMEA is most commonly used in the Improve step of the DMAIC method to improve the effectiveness of a proposed solution, but it is also helpful in the Recognize step for identifying improvement opportunities, and in the Measure step for determining what data to collect and where to collect it.

What does it do?

- Follows the steps of the process and identifies where problems might occur
- Scores potential problems based on their probability of occurrence, severity, and ability to be detected
- Based on the scores mentioned above, helps to determine where countermeasures are necessary to avoid problems
- Allows re-scoring of the problem after you have put countermeasures in place

How do I do it?

1. **List the process steps in the first column of a chart like the one below**

Sample FMEA Chart

Project _____ Team _____ Date _____ (original) / _____ (revised)

Item or Process Step	Potential Failure Mode	Potential Effect(s) of Failure	Severity	Potential Cause(s)	Occurrence	Current Controls	Detection	RPN	Recommended Action	Responsibility and Target Date	"After" Action Taken	Severity	Occurrence	Detection	RPN

Total Risk Priority Number =

"After" Risk Priority Number =

112   Failure Mode/Effects Analysis ©2002 GOAL/QPC

2. **For each process step, brainstorm potential failure modes**—ways in which the product, service, or process might fail (e.g., jams, sputters, freezes or slows up, is unreadable)

3. **Identify the potential consequences or effects of each failure** (e.g., defective product, wrong information, delays) and rate their severity

4. **Identify causes of the effects and rate their likelihood of occurrence**

5. **Rate your ability to detect each failure mode (in the Detection column)**

6. **Multiply the three numbers (severity, occurrence, and detection) together to determine the risk of each failure mode. This is represented in the chart by a risk priority number, or RPN.**
   - RPN = severity × occurrence × detection

7. **Identify ways to reduce or eliminate risk associated with high RPNs**

8. **Re-score those failures after you put countermeasures in place**

   Tip There might be multiple failures for each step and multiple effects for each failure. Score each separately.

   Tip Develop your own scales for severity, occurrence, and detection or use the sample scales shown on the next page.

Sample Severity, Occurrence, & Detection Scales

Severity = likely impact of the failure

	Rating	Criteria: A failure could . . .
Bad	10	Injure a customer or employee
	9	Be illegal
	8	Render the product or service unfit for use
	7	Cause extreme customer dissatisfaction
	6	Result in partial malfunction
	5	Cause a loss of performance likely to result in a complaint
	4	Cause minor performance loss
	3	Cause a minor nuisance; can be overcome with no loss
	2	Be unnoticed; minor effect on performance
Good	1	Be unnoticed and not affect the performance

Occurrence = how often the cause will occur

	Rating	Time Period	Probability
Bad	10	More than once per day	> 30%
	9	Once every 3–4 days	< 30%
	8	Once per week	< 5%
	7	Once per month	< 1%
	6	Once every 3 months	< .03%
	5	Once every 6 months	< 1 per 10,000
	4	Once per year	< 6 per 100,000
	3	Once every 1–3 years	< 6 per million
	2	Once every 3–6 years	< 3 per 10 million
Good	1	Once every 6–100 years	< 2 per billion

Detection = how likely we are to know if the cause has occurred

	Rating	Definition
Bad	10	Defect caused by failure is not detectable
	9	Occasional units are checked for defects
	8	Units are systematically sampled and inspected
	7	All units are manually inspected
	6	Manual inspection with mistake-proofing modifications
	5	Process is monitored via statistical process control (SPC) and manually inspected
	4	SPC used, with an immediate reaction to out-of-control conditions
	3	SPC as above, with 100% inspection surrounding out-of-control conditions
	2	All units are automatically inspected
Good	1	Defect is obvious and can be kept from affecting customer

Variations

Error Mode and Effects Analysis (EMEA) is sometimes used to track processes in which the primary failures are human errors. With EMEA, errors, rather than failures, are tracked and scored.

Flowchart
Picturing the process

Why use it?

To allow a team to identify the actual flow or sequence of events in a process that any product or service follows. Flowcharts can be applied to anything from the travels of an invoice or the flow of materials, to the steps in making a sale or servicing a product.

What does it do?

- Shows unexpected complexity, problem areas, redundancy, unnecessary loops, and where simplification and standardization may be possible
- Compares and contrasts the actual versus the ideal flow of a process to identify improvement opportunities
- Allows a team to come to agreement on the steps of the process and to examine which activities may impact the process performance
- Identifies locations where additional data can be collected and investigated
- Serves as a training aid to understand the complete process

How do I do it?

1. **Determine the frame or boundaries of the process**
   - Clearly define where the process under study starts (input) and ends (final output).
   - Team members should agree to the level of detail they must show on the Flowchart to clearly understand the process and identify problem areas.

- The Flowchart can be a simple macro-flowchart showing only sufficient information to understand the general process flow, or it might be detailed to show every finite action and decision point. The team might start out with a macro-flowchart and then add in detail later or only where it is needed.

2. Determine the steps in the process
- Brainstorm a list of all major activities, inputs, outputs, and decisions on a flipchart sheet from the beginning of the process to the end.

3. Sequence the steps
- Arrange the steps in the order they are carried out. Use Post-it® Notes so you can move them around. Don't draw in the arrows yet.

Tip Unless you are flowcharting a new process, sequence what *is*, not what *should be* or the ideal. This may be difficult at first but is necessary to see where the probable causes of the problems are in the process.

4. Draw the Flowchart using the appropriate symbols

An oval is used to show the materials, information, or action (inputs) to start the process or to show the results at the end (output) of the process.

A box or rectangle is used to show a task or activity performed in the process. Although multiple arrows may come into each box, usually only one output or arrow leaves each activity box.

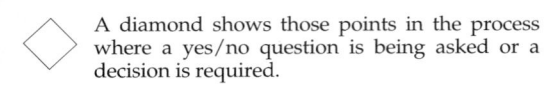

⬦ A diamond shows those points in the process where a yes/no question is being asked or a decision is required.

Ⓐ A circle with either a letter or a number identifies a break in the Flowchart and is continued elsewhere on the same page or another page.

→ Arrows show the direction or flow of the process.

- Keep the Flowchart simple using the basic symbols listed above. As your experience grows, use other, more graphic symbols to represent the steps. Other symbols sometimes used include:
  - A half or torn sheet of paper for a report completed and/or filed.
  - A can or computer tape wheel for data entry into a computer database.
  - A large "D" or half circle to identify places in the process where there is a delay or wait for further action.
- Be consistent in the level of detail shown.
  - A macro-level flowchart will show key action steps but no decision boxes.
  - An intermediate-level flowchart will show action and decision points.
  - A micro-level flowchart will show minute detail.
- Label each process step using words that are understandable to everyone.
- Add arrows to show the direction of the flow of steps in the process. Although it is not a rule, if you show all "yes" choices branching down and "no" choices branching to the left, it is easier to

follow the process. Preferences and space will later dictate direction.
- Don't forget to identify your work. Include the title of your process, the date the diagram was made, and the names of the team members.

5. Test the Flowchart for completeness
- Are the symbols used correctly?
- Are the process steps (inputs, outputs, actions, decisions, waits/delays) identified clearly?
- Make sure every feedback loop is closed, i.e., every path takes you either back to or ahead to another step.
- Check that every continuation point has a corresponding point elsewhere in the Flowchart or on another page of the Flowchart.
- There is usually only one output arrow out of an activity box. If there is more than one arrow, you may need a decision diamond.
- Validate the Flowchart with people who are not on the team and who carry out the process actions. Highlight additions or deletions they recommend. Bring these back to the team to discuss and incorporate into the final Flowchart.

6. Finalize the Flowchart
- Is this process being run the way it should be?
- Are people following the process as charted?
- Are there obvious complexities or redundancies that can be reduced or eliminated?
- How different is the current process from an ideal one? Draw an ideal Flowchart. Compare the two (current versus ideal) to identify discrepancies and opportunities for improvements.

Flowchart

Proposed Patient Appointment Procedure

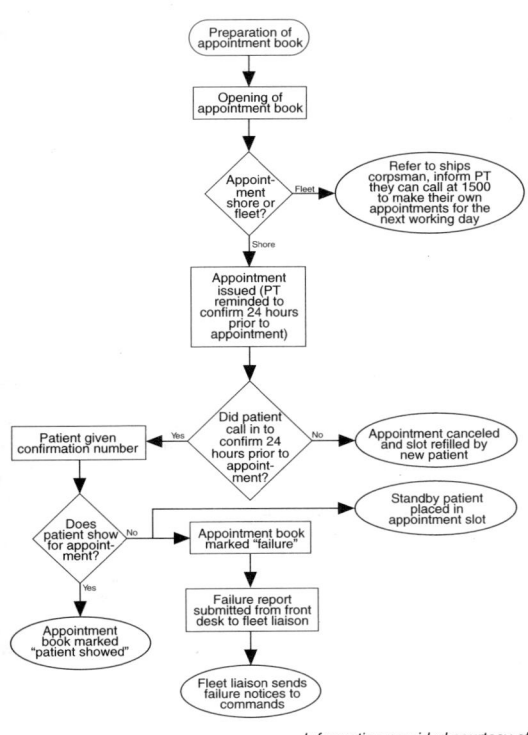

```
Preparation of appointment book
         │
         ▼
Opening of appointment book
         │
         ▼
   Appointment ──Fleet──▶ Refer to ships corpsman, inform PT
   shore or              they can call at 1500 to make their
    fleet?               own appointments for the next working day
         │
       Shore
         ▼
Appointment issued (PT reminded to
confirm 24 hours prior to appointment)
         │
         ▼
   Did patient call in to ──No──▶ Appointment canceled
   confirm 24 hours prior          and slot refilled by
   to appointment?                 new patient
         │
        Yes
         ▼
Patient given confirmation number
         │
         ▼
   Does patient show ──No──▶ Appointment book ──▶ Standby patient placed
   for appointment?          marked "failure"      in appointment slot
         │                        │
        Yes                       ▼
         ▼                 Failure report submitted from
Appointment book           front desk to fleet liaison
marked "patient showed"          │
                                 ▼
                          Fleet liaison sends failure
                          notices to commands
```

Information provided courtesy of
U.S. Navy, Naval Dental Center, San Diego

Variations

The type of Flowchart just described is sometimes referred to as a "detailed" flowchart because it includes, in detail, the inputs, activities, decision points, and outputs of any process. Four other forms, described below, are also useful.

Macro-Flowchart

Refer to the third bulleted item in Step 1 of this section for a description. For a graphic example, see page 119 of *The Memory Jogger™ II*.

Top-Down Flowchart

This chart is a picture of the major steps in a work process. It minimizes the detail to focus only on those steps essential to the process. It usually does not include inspection, rework, and other steps that result in quality problems. Teams sometimes study the top-down flowchart to look for ways to simplify or reduce the number of steps to make the process more efficient and effective.

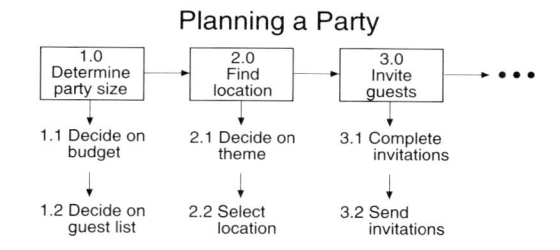

Planning a Party

1.0 Determine party size	2.0 Find location	3.0 Invite guests	▶ • • •
1.1 Decide on budget	2.1 Decide on theme	3.1 Complete invitations	
1.2 Decide on guest list	2.2 Select location	3.2 Send invitations	

Deployment Flowchart

This chart shows the people or departments responsible and the flow of the process steps or tasks they are assigned. It is useful to clarify roles and track accountability as well as to indicate dependencies in the sequence of events.

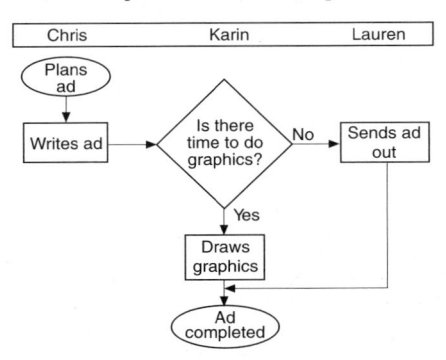

```
| Chris        | Karin              | Lauren     |

(Plans ad)
    |
    v
[Writes ad] --> <Is there time to do graphics?> --No--> [Sends ad out]
                        |                                     |
                       Yes                                    |
                        v                                     |
                 [Draws graphics]                             |
                        |                                     |
                        v                                     |
                   (Ad completed) <--------------------------+
```

Opportunity Flowchart

This type of chart helps you improve a process by differentiating its value-added steps from its non-value-added steps. *Value-added steps* are those that are essential for producing the product or service and are needed even if the process were to run perfectly every time. *Non-value-added steps* are those that are added to a process because defects, errors, and omissions occur or because of worry that they might occur.

Remember these tips when constructing an Opportunity Flowchart: Divide a page into two sections. The value-added section should be smaller than the non-value-added section. Time flows down the page. Join two value-added steps with an arrow only if there are no non-value-added steps in between.

A Sample Opportunity Flowchart

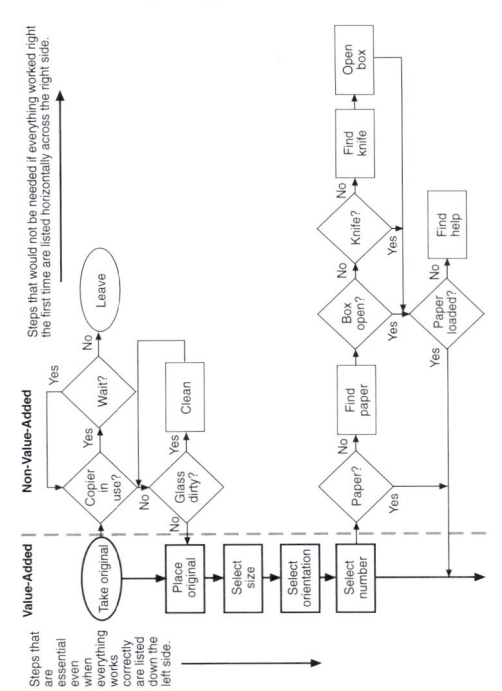

Steps that would not be needed if everything worked right the first time are listed horizontally across the right side.

Non-Value-Added

Value-Added

Steps that are essential even when everything works correctly are listed down the left side.

Flow: Take original → (Copier in use? Yes → Wait? Yes → Leave; No) → (Glass dirty? Yes → Clean; No) → Place original → Select size → Select orientation → Select number → (Paper? No → Find paper; Yes) → (Box open? Yes; No → Knife? Yes → Find knife; No → Open box) → (Paper loaded? Yes; No → Find help)

Workflow Flowchart

This type of chart is used to show the flow of people, materials, paperwork, etc., within a work setting. When redundancies, duplications, and unnecessary complexities are identified in a path, people can take action to reduce or eliminate these problems.

©2002 GOAL/QPC

Focused Problem Statement
Narrowing the problem definition

Why use it?

To narrow the focus of a problem so that you can use your time and resources most effectively in finding a solution.

What does it do?

- Describes specifically what occurs, when or under what circumstances it occurs, and/or who is involved
- Prevents a team from getting bogged down trying to do too much at once
- Alleviates the difficulties of getting beyond general issues, which are harder to tackle than specific ones
- Keeps the team motivated and focused

Narrowing a Problem Statement

Poor service at the Royal Treatment Hotel.

X						
Broad or vague		Somewhat focused		Narrow focus		

What: *Poor service*

Late room service at the Royal Treatment Hotel.

			X			
Broad or vague		Somewhat focused		Narrow focus		

What: *Poor service*
What type of service: *Room service*
What about the service: *It is late*

Late room service between 6 a.m. and 8 a.m. on weekdays at the Royal Treatment Hotel.

						X
Broad or vague		Somewhat focused		Narrow focus		

What: *Poor service*
What type of service: *Room service*
What about the service: *It is late*
When is this problem the greatest:
Between 6 a.m. and 8 a.m. on weekdays

How do I do it?

1. Review the problem statement on your charter
2. Review the data from the Measure step of the DMAIC method to get clues about the specifics (i.e., who, what, when, where, which) of the problem you are addressing
3. Complete a worksheet like the one on the next page using the questions provided to develop a Focused Problem Statement

Creating a Focused Problem Statement

Focus your problem by asking who, what, when, where, and which.

Use the questions on the left to help you write a Focused Problem Statement.

_____
_____
_____
_____
_____

What is the nature of the problem?

- What happens?
- What type of problem is it?
- What do we know about it?

Where does the problem occur?

- Physical location
- Step in the process

Put an X where you think your problem statement falls on the scale.

Broad or vague	Somewhat focused	Narrow focus

When does the problem occur?

- Day, time of day, shift, month, season, annual cycle
- When doesn't it occur?
- When is the problem greatest?

If your problem statement falls in the shaded area, what data or other information can you collect to help make your problem statement more focused?

_____
_____
_____
_____
_____

Who is involved?

- Which customers?
- Which suppliers?
- Who else is involved?

Tip If you have no answers or vague answers to the questions on the worksheet, you might need to do more work in the Measure step of the DMAIC method before proceeding with the Analyze step.

Tip There are no rules that tell you when a problem is focused enough. Trying to develop a Focused Problem Statement is a balancing act. You want to have enough focus so that it is easy to identify causes and take effective action, but you don't want to spend so much time, effort, and money on this step that you never get around to taking action! At some point, therefore, you have to decide whether the cost of getting more data and more focus is worth the investment.

Sample Focused Problem Statements

Situation	Broad, vague →	Somewhat focused →	Narrow focus
Product development	Missed deadlines	New products routinely miss target launch dates	New CD-ROM products routinely miss target launch dates by three months
Accounts receivable	Late payments	Late payments from Service A customers	Late payments from international customers of Service A
Injuries	Muscle strains	High number of muscle strains among warehouse personnel	High number of back-muscle strains among material handlers

A Comparison of Problem Statements

Takes too long to close the books at the end of the month

X				
Broad or vague		Somewhat focused		Narrow focus

What: *Closing the books*

Does not include:
Which departments have problems

When the problem started

Whether the problem happens all the time or comes and goes

What types of financial records have the biggest delays

Increase in the number of open inner packs of Fiber Flakes cereal from the #3 sealing machine during the last three days

				X
Broad or vague		Somewhat focused		Narrow focus

What product is involved: *Fiber Flakes cereal*

What problem occurs: *Increase in open packs*

Which packs: *Inner packs*

Where does problem occur: *Sealing machine #3*

When did problem occur: *The last three days*

Inaccurate hospital bills for surgery patients at City Hospital

		X		
Broad or vague		Somewhat focused		Narrow focus

What: *Inaccurate bills*

Which patients: *Surgery patients*

Where: *City Hospital*

Does not include:
What types of inaccuracies?

What kinds of surgeries?

When did the problem start?

---

128 Focused Problem Statement ©2002 GOAL/QPC

Histogram
Process centering, spread, and shape

Why use it?
To summarize data from a process that has been collected over a period of time, and graphically present its frequency distribution in bar form.

What does it do?
- Displays large amounts of data that are difficult to interpret in tabular form
- Shows the relative frequency of occurrence of the various data values
- Reveals the centering, variation, and shape of the data
- Illustrates quickly the underlying distribution of the data
- Provides useful information for predicting future performance of the process
- Helps to indicate if there has been a change in the process
- Helps answer the question "Is the process capable of meeting my customer requirements?"

How do I do it?

1. **Decide on the process measure**

    - The data should be variable data, i.e., measured on a continuous scale. For example: temperature, time, dimensions, weight, speed.

2. Gather data

- Collect at least 50 to 100 data points if you plan on looking for patterns and calculating the distribution's centering (mean), spread (variation), and shape. You might also consider collecting data for a specified period of time: hour, shift, day, week, etc.
- Use historical data to find patterns or to use as a baseline measure of past performance.

3. Prepare a frequency table from the data

a) Count the number of data points, n, in the sample.

9.9	9.3	10.2	9.4	10.1	9.6	9.9	10.1	9.8
9.8	9.8	10.1	9.9	9.7	9.8	9.9	10.0	9.6
9.7	9.4	9.6	10.0	9.8	9.9	10.1	10.4	10.0
10.2	10.1	9.8	10.1	10.3	10.0	10.2	9.8	10.7
9.9	10.7	9.3	10.3	9.9	9.8	10.3	9.5	9.9
9.3	10.2	9.2	9.9	9.7	9.9	9.8	9.5	9.4
9.0	9.5	9.7	9.7	9.8	9.8	9.3	9.6	9.7
10.0	9.7	9.4	9.8	9.4	9.6	10.0	10.3	9.8
9.5	9.7	10.6	9.5	10.1	10.0	9.8	10.1	9.6
9.6	9.4	10.1	9.5	10.1	10.2	9.8	9.5	9.3
10.3	9.6	9.7	9.7	10.1	9.8	9.7	10.0	10.0
9.5	9.5	9.8	9.9	9.2	10.0	10.0	9.7	9.7
9.9	10.4	9.3	9.6	10.2	9.7	9.7	9.7	10.7
9.9	10.2	9.8	9.3	9.6	9.5	9.6	10.7	

In this example, there are 125 data points, n = 125.

b) Determine the range, R, for the entire sample.

The range is the smallest value in the set of data subtracted from the largest value. For our example:

$$R = X_{max} - X_{min} = 10.7 - 9.0 = 1.7$$

c) Determine the number of class intervals, k, needed.

130 Histogram ©2002 GOAL/QPC

- Method 1: Take the square root of the total number of data points and round to the nearest whole number.

  $k = \sqrt{125} = 11.18 = 11$ intervals

- Method 2: Use the table below to provide a guideline for dividing your sample into a reasonable number of classes.

Number of Data Points	Number of Classes (k)
Under 50	5 – 7
50 – 100	6 – 10
100 – 250	7 – 12
Over 250	10 – 20

For our example, 125 data points would be divided into 7–12 class intervals.

Tip These two methods are general rules of thumb for determining class intervals. In both methods, consider using k = 10 class intervals for ease of "mental" calculation.

Tip The number of intervals can influence the pattern of the sample. Too few intervals will produce a tight, high pattern. Too many intervals will produce a spread-out, flat pattern.

d) Determine the class width, H.

- The formula for this is:

  $H = \dfrac{R}{k} = \dfrac{1.7}{10} = .17$

- Round your number to the nearest value with the same decimal numbers as the original sample. In our example, we would round up to .20. It is useful to have intervals defined to one more decimal place than the data collected.

e) Determine the class boundaries, or end points.

- Use the smallest individual measurement in the sample, or round to the next appropriate lowest round number. This will be the lower end point for the *first* class interval. In our example this would be 9.0.
- Add the class width, H, to the lower end point. This will be the lower end point for the *next* class interval. For our example:

    9.0 + H = 9.0 + .20 = 9.20

Thus, the first class interval would be 9.00 and everything up to, *but not including*, 9.20; that is, 9.00 through 9.19. The second class interval would begin at 9.20 and be everything up to, but not including, 9.40.

Tip Each class interval must be *mutually exclusive*; that is, every data point will fit into *one and only one* class interval.

- Consecutively add the class width to the lowest class boundary until the k class intervals and/or the range of all the numbers are obtained.

f) Construct the frequency table based on the values you computed in item "e."

A frequency table based on the data from our example is shown below.

Class #	Class Boundaries	Mid-Point	Frequency	Total
1	9.00-9.19	9.1	I	1
2	9.20-9.39	9.3	ℍℍ IIII	9
3	9.40-9.59	9.5	ℍℍ ℍℍ ℍℍ I	16
4	9.60-9.79	9.7	ℍℍ ℍℍ ℍℍ ℍℍ ℍℍ II	27
5	9.80-9.99	9.9	ℍℍ ℍℍ ℍℍ ℍℍ ℍℍ ℍℍ I	31
6	10.00-10.19	10.1	ℍℍ ℍℍ ℍℍ ℍℍ II	22
7	10.20-10.39	10.3	ℍℍ ℍℍ II	12
8	10.40-10.59	10.5	II	2
9	10.60-10.79	10.7	ℍℍ	5
10	10.80-10.99	10.9		0

4. Draw a Histogram from the frequency table

- On the vertical line (y axis), draw the frequency (count) scale to cover class interval with the highest frequency count.
- On the horizontal line (x axis), draw the scale related to the variable you are measuring.
- For each class interval, draw a bar with the height equal to the frequency tally of that class.

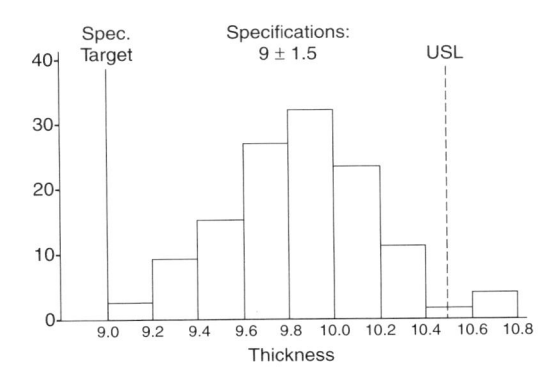

5. Interpret the Histogram

a) *Centering.* Where is the distribution centered? Is the process running too high? Too low?

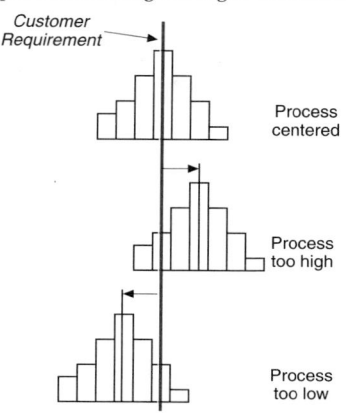

- Process centered (Customer Requirement)
- Process too high
- Process too low

b) *Variation.* What is the variation or spread of the data? Is it too variable?

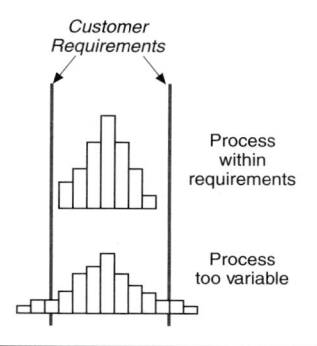

- Process within requirements (Customer Requirements)
- Process too variable

134 Histogram

c) *Shape*. What is the shape? Does it look like a normal, bell-shaped distribution? Is it positively or negatively skewed; that is, more data values to the left or to the right? Are there twin (bi-modal) or multiple peaks?

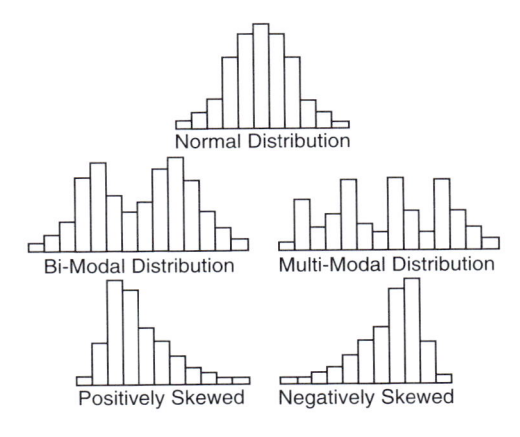

Normal Distribution

Bi-Modal Distribution   Multi-Modal Distribution

Positively Skewed   Negatively Skewed

Tip Some processes are naturally skewed; don't expect every distribution to follow a bell-shaped curve.

Tip Always look for twin or multiple peaks indicating that the data is coming from two or more different sources, e.g., shifts, machines, people, suppliers. If this is evident, stratify the data.

d) *Process Capability*. Compare the results of your Histogram to your customer requirements or specifications. Is your process capable of meeting the requirements, i.e., is the Histogram centered on the target and within the specification limits?

Centering and Spread Compared to Customer Target and Limits

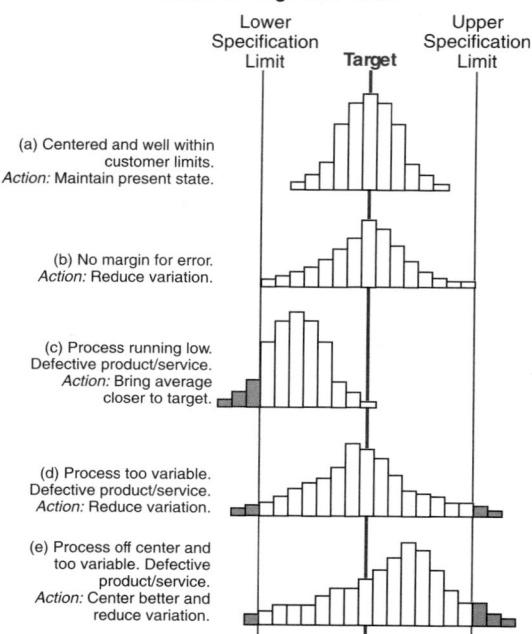

Lower Specification Limit — **Target** — **Upper Specification Limit**

(a) Centered and well within customer limits.
Action: Maintain present state.

(b) No margin for error.
Action: Reduce variation.

(c) Process running low. Defective product/service.
Action: Bring average closer to target.

(d) Process too variable. Defective product/service.
Action: Reduce variation.

(e) Process off center and too variable. Defective product/service.
Action: Center better and reduce variation.

Tip Get suspicious of the accuracy of the data if the Histogram suddenly stops at one point (such as a specification limit) without some previous decline in the data. It could indicate that defective product is being sorted out and is not included in the sample.

Tip The Histogram is related to the Control Chart. Like a Control Chart, a normally distributed Histogram will have almost all its values within ±3 standard deviations of the mean. See page 132 of *The Memory Jogger™ II* for an illustration of this.

Variations

Stem & Leaf Plot

This plot is a cross between a frequency distribution and a Histogram. It exhibits the shape of a Histogram, but preserves the original data values—one of its key benefits! Data is easily recorded by writing the trailing digits in the appropriate row of leading digits.

```
.05|7          Data as              .05|7          Data rank-
.06|4          collected            .06|4          ordered
.07|5 7                             .07|5 7
.08|1 9 3 9                         .08|1 3 9 9
.09|7 4 8 2 6 9 4                   .09|2 4 4 6 7 8 9
.10|7 2 0 4 3 5 9                   .10|0 2 3 4 5 7 9
.11|3 1 9 3 7 3 8 6 6               .11|1 3 3 3 6 6 7 8 9
.12|4 8 0 8 9 0 5                   .12|0 0 4 5 8 8 9
.13|2 5 2 7 7 6                     .13|2 2 5 6 7 7
.14|0 3 6 9                         .14|0 3 6 9
.15|4 7                             .15|4 7
.16|4 7                             .16|4 7
```

In this example, the smallest value is .057, and the largest value is .164. Using such a plot, it is easy to find the median and range of the data.

- Median = middle data value (or average of the two middle values) when the data is ranked from smallest to largest.

For this example, there are 52 data points. Therefore, the average of the 26th and 27th value will give the median value.

Median = (.113 + .116)/2 = .1145

- Range = Highest value – lowest value = .164 – .057 = .107

Histogram
Time Distribution of Calls

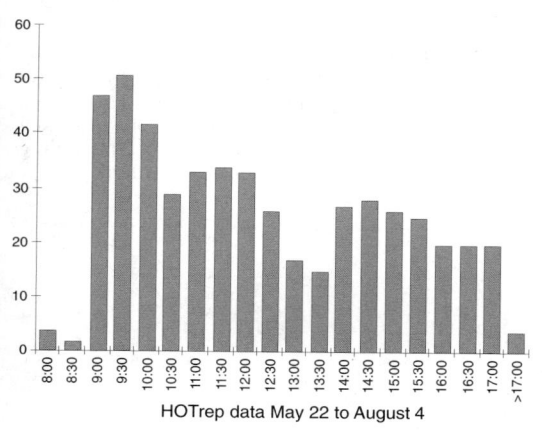

HOTrep data May 22 to August 4

Information provided courtesy of SmithKline Beecham

Note: The Histogram identified three peak calling periods at the beginning of the workday and before and after the traditional lunch hour. This can help the HOTreps synchronize staffing with their customer needs.

Dot Plot

Like a Histogram, a Dot Plot illustrates the frequency of occurrences, except dots are used to represent frequency on the chart instead of bars.

Time to Fill Walk-In Prescriptions

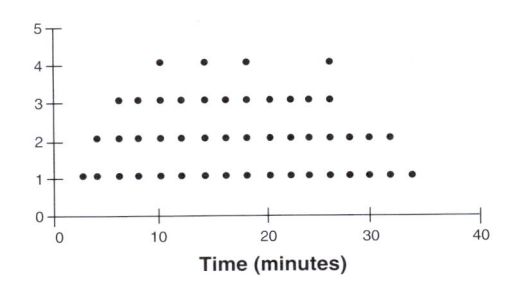

Stratifying Frequency Diagrams

As described in the Data Collection section, stratification can provide useful insight into what is actually happening in a process. When displaying stratified data, you should code the data points to visually separate the various data groups. You can use the following methods to code your data:

- Different labels, colors, or symbols
- Different plots side by side

A Sample Stratified Frequency Diagram

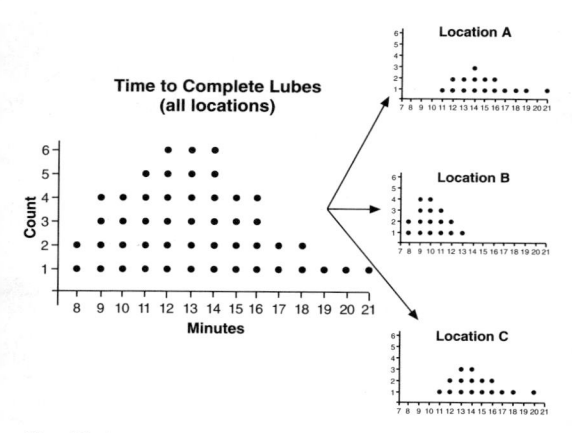

Time to Complete Lubes (all locations)

Location A

Location B

Location C

Box Plot

A Box Plot (also known as a Box and Whisker Plot) is particularly helpful for showing the distribution of data. It shows similar information as the Dot Plot and has a few additional features. In this example, a team was looking at call volumes by day of the week. This data is shown on the next page in the form of a Box Plot.

The outline of the box on the Box Plot indicates the middle 50% of the data (the middle two quartiles). The line inside the box represents the median. The lines extending on either side of the box, called whiskers, represent an upper limit and a lower limit. These limits are based on one and one-half times the length of the box added to either side of the box (if there are values that extreme) or the highest or lowest value. The asterisk represents any values that lie beyond the limits.

Sample Box Plots

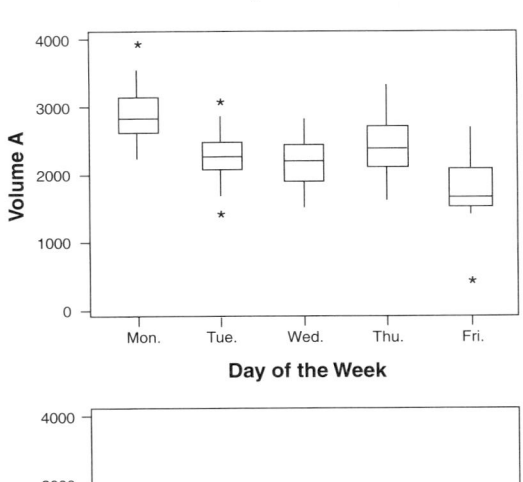

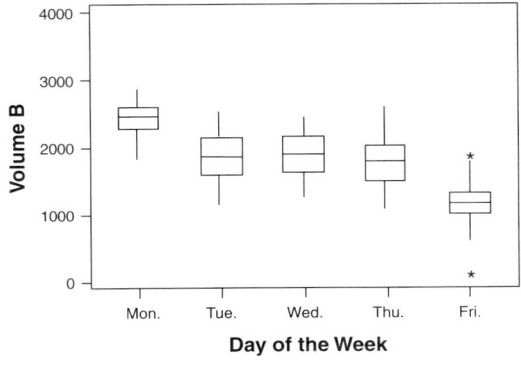

Volume A vs **Day of the Week** (Mon., Tue., Wed., Thu., Fri.)

Volume B vs **Day of the Week** (Mon., Tue., Wed., Thu., Fri.)

Hypothesis Testing
Checking for differences

Why use it?
Hypothesis testing is used to help determine if the variation between groups of data is due to true differences between the groups or is the result of *common-cause variation*, which is the natural variation in a process. This tool is most commonly used in the Analyze step of the DMAIC method to determine if different levels of a discrete process setting (x) result in significant differences in the output (y). An example would be "Do different regions of the country have different defect levels?" This tool is also used in the Improve step of the DMAIC method to prove a statistically significant difference in "before" and "after" data.

What does it do?
- Identifies whether a particular discrete x has an effect on the y
- Checks for the statistical significance of differences. In other words, it helps determine if the difference observed between groups is bigger than what you would expect from common-cause variation alone.
- Gives a p-value, which is the probability that a difference you observe is as big as it is only because of common-cause variation
- Can be used to compare two or more groups of data, such as "before" and "after" data

How do I do it?

1. **Collect and plot the data**
   - You might want to make stratified histograms for the different data groups so you can get a feel for the data. Here, data collected on time to close a loan is plotted for three different loan types (A, B, and C).

   Here the hypothesis being tested is that the three different types of loans take the same amount of time to close. The hypothesis test will tell us the likelihood of that being true, even though the data plot is inconclusive.

   A Hypothesis-Testing Data Plot

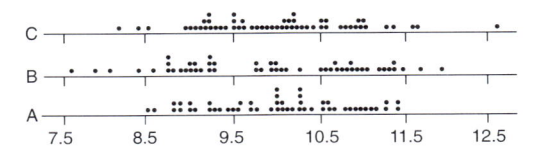

2. **Select the appropriate test**
   - The type of hypothesis test you use depends on the type of data you have. Use hypothesis tests when the x is discrete. (See the table at left on the next page. Use the flowchart on the right as a guide for selecting the appropriate type of hypothesis test to use.)

   Since the y in this example (time to close) is continuous and the x (loan type) is discrete, Analysis of Variance is the appropriate type of test to select.

Hypothesis Testing

Which Hypothesis Test to Use?

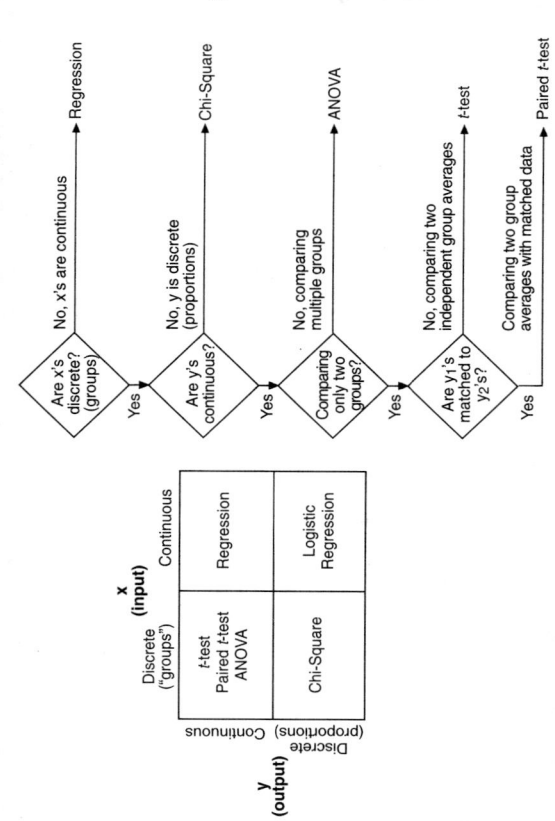

	x (input)	
	Discrete ("groups")	Continuous
y (output) Continuous	t-test Paired t-test ANOVA	Regression
Discrete (proportions)	Chi-Square	Logistic Regression

Decision flow:

- Are x's discrete? (groups)
  - No, x's are continuous → **Regression**
  - Yes → Are y's continuous?
    - No, y is discrete (proportions) → **Chi-Square**
    - Yes → Comparing only two groups?
      - No, comparing multiple groups → **ANOVA**
      - Yes → Are y_1's matched to y_2's?
        - No, comparing two independent group averages → **t-test**
        - Yes, comparing two group averages with matched data → **Paired t-test**

144 Hypothesis Testing   ©2002 GOAL/QPC

3. Analyze the data

- Hypothesis tests compare observed differences between groups.
- Hypothesis tests give a p-value. This value equals the probability of obtaining the observed difference given that the "true" difference is zero.
- A p-value can range from 0.0 to 1.0 (i.e., from a 0% chance to a 100% chance).
- Usually, a p-value of less than .05 indicates that a difference is significant. When you get a p-value of less than .05, then conclude there is little chance that the true difference is zero.
- When a difference is significant, you can conclude that the data groups are different. You can then investigate x as a driver of y or conclude there is a difference in the "before" and "after" data.

For this example, the averages of the three groups are as follows: A = 10.02, B = 9.86, and C = 10.03. The hypothesis test gives a p-value of 0.56—larger than 0.05, which indicates that the differences in the group averages are small. This means that there is not enough evidence to conclude that the different loan types have different cycle times.

Tip Hypothesis tests often require you to gather a lot of data to observe a significant difference. Work with your Six Sigma Expert or Master Six Sigma Expert to determine the power of your test and to detect the size difference you are looking for. You might need to collect additional data to see the difference you desire.

Tip Hypothesis tests are so named because they start with what is called a *null hypothesis* and set out to prove or disprove it. The null hypothesis states that there is no difference between the groups. This null hypothesis is assumed to be true until it is disproven with data. If the result of the test proves to be significant (p < .05), the null hypothesis is declared to be untrue.

Tip When performing Analysis of Variance (ANOVA) testing, you should also perform an additional hypothesis test for equal variance in the subgroups. The ANOVA assumes equal variances. Your Six Sigma Expert or Master Six Sigma Expert can help you draw conclusions if this assumption is not met.

Variations

Many statistical procedures have built-in hypothesis tests. For example, in regression analysis (see page 214 for details), p-values are given on a slope. These values come from a test of the null hypothesis that the slope is zero (i.e., there is no difference in slope).

Interrelationship Digraph (ID)
Looking for drivers & outcomes

Why use it?

To allow a team to systematically identify, analyze, and classify the cause-and-effect relationships that exist among all critical issues so that key drivers or outcomes can become the heart of an effective solution.

What does it do?

- Encourages team members to think in multiple directions rather than linearly
- Explores the cause-and-effect relationships among all the issues, including the most controversial
- Allows the key issues to emerge naturally rather than allowing the issues to be forced by a dominant or powerful team member
- Systematically surfaces the basic assumptions and reasons for disagreements among team members
- Allows a team to identify root cause(s) even when credible data doesn't exist

How do I do it?

1. **Agree on the issue/problem statement**

> What are the issues related to reducing litter?

- If using an original statement (i.e., it didn't come from a previous tool or discussion), create a com-

plete sentence that is clearly understood and agreed on by team members.
- If using input from other tools, such as an Affinity Diagram, make sure that the goal under discussion is still the same and clearly understood.

2. **Assemble the right team**
    - The ID requires more intimate knowledge of the subject under discussion than is needed for the Affinity. This is important if the final cause-and-effect patterns are to be credible.
    - The ideal team size is generally 4–6 people. However, this number can be increased as long as the issues are still visible and the meeting is well facilitated to encourage participation and maintain focus.

3. **Lay out all of the ideas/issue cards that have either been brought from other tools or brainstormed**
    - Arrange 5–25 cards or notes in a large circular pattern, leaving as much space as possible for drawing arrows. Use large, bold printing, including a large number or letter on each idea for quick reference later in the process.

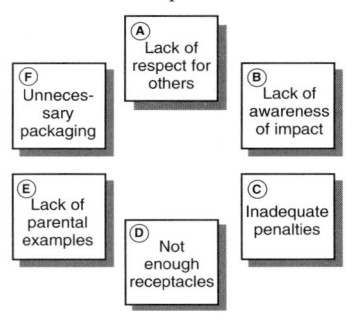

(A) Lack of respect for others
(B) Lack of awareness of impact
(C) Inadequate penalties
(D) Not enough receptacles
(E) Lack of parental examples
(F) Unnecessary packaging

148 Interrelationship Digraph ©2002 GOAL/QPC

4. Look for cause/influence relationships among all of the ideas and draw relationship arrows

- Choose any of the ideas as a starting point. If all of the ideas are numbered or lettered, work through them in sequence.
- An outgoing arrow from an idea indicates that it is the stronger cause or influence.

Ask of each combination:
1) Is there a cause/influence relationship?
2) If yes, which direction of cause/influence is stronger?

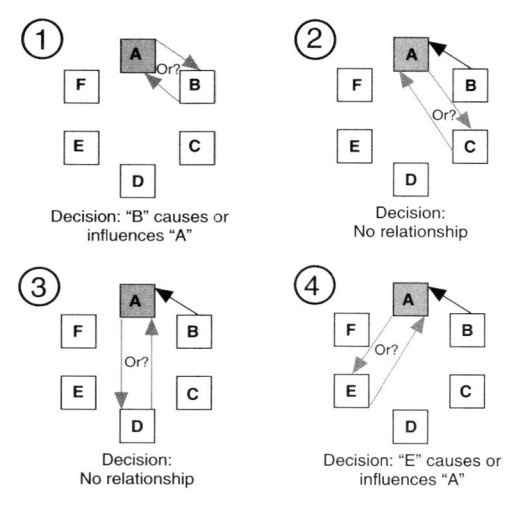

① Decision: "B" causes or influences "A"

② Decision: No relationship

③ Decision: No relationship

④ Decision: "E" causes or influences "A"

Continued next page

⑤

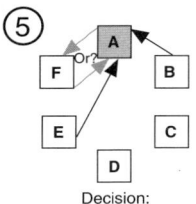

Decision:
No relationship.
"A" is completed.

⑥

Decision: "B" causes or
influences "C."
**Now begin with "B" and repeat the
questions for all remaining
combinations.**

Tip Draw only one-way relationship arrows in the direction of the stronger cause or influence. Make a decision on the stronger direction. ***Do not draw two-headed arrows.***

5. **Review and revise the first-round ID**
   - Get additional input from people who are not on the team to confirm or modify the team's work. Either bring the paper version to others or reproduce it using available software. Use a different-size print or a color marker to make additions or deletions.

6. **Tally the number of outgoing and incoming arrows and select key items for further planning**
   - Record and clearly mark next to each issue the number of arrows going in and out of it.
   - Find the item(s) with the highest number of *outgoing arrows* and the item(s) with the highest number of *incoming arrows*.
   - *Outgoing arrows*. A high number of outgoing arrows indicates an item that is a root cause or driver. This is *generally* the issue that teams tackle first.

- *Incoming arrows.* A high number of incoming arrows indicates an item that is a key outcome. This can become a focus for planning either as a meaningful measure of overall success or as a redefinition of the original issue under discussion.

   Tip Use common sense when you select the most critical issues to focus on. Issues with very close tallies must be reviewed carefully, but in the end it is a judgment call, not science.

7. **Draw the final ID**
   - Identify visually both the *key drivers* (greatest number of outgoing arrows) and the *key outcomes* (greatest number of incoming arrows). Typical methods are double boxes or bold boxes.

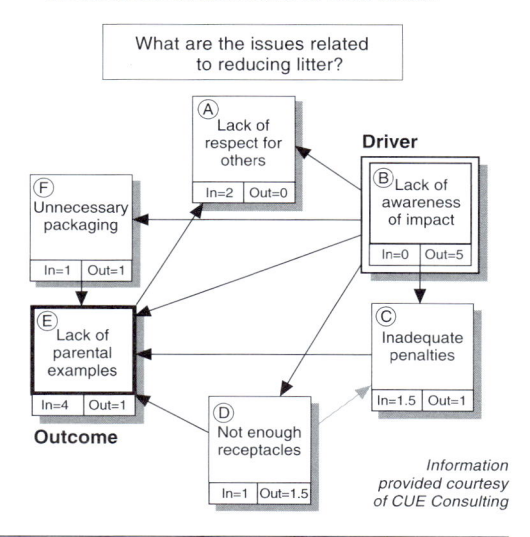

What are the issues related to reducing litter?

- Ⓐ Lack of respect for others — In=2 | Out=0
- Ⓑ Lack of awareness of impact — In=0 | Out=5 — **Driver**
- Ⓒ Inadequate penalties — In=1.5 | Out=1
- Ⓓ Not enough receptacles — In=1 | Out=1.5
- Ⓔ Lack of parental examples — In=4 | Out=1 — **Outcome**
- Ⓕ Unnecessary packaging — In=1 | Out=1

Information provided courtesy of CUE Consulting

©2002 GOAL/QPC   Interrelationship Digraph 151

Variations

When it is necessary to create a more orderly display of all of the relationships, a matrix format is very effective. The vertical (up) arrow is a driving cause, and the horizontal (side) arrow is an effect. The example below has added symbols indicating the strength of the relationships.

The "total" column is the sum of all of the "relationship strengths" in each row. This shows that you are working on those items that have the strongest effect on the greatest number of issues.

ID – Matrix Format

	Logistic Support	Customer Satisfaction	Education & Training	Personnel Incentives	Leadership	Cause /Driver ↑	Result/ Rider ←	Total
Logistic Support	■	⊙ ↑	○ ↑	△ ↑	○ ↑	3	1	16
Customer Satisfaction	⊙ ←	■	○ ←	⊙ ←	○ ←	0	4	24
Education & Training	○ ←	○ ↑	■	○ ↑	⊙ ←	2	2	18
Personnel Incentives	△ ←	⊙ ↑	○ ↑	■	⊙ ←	1	3	22
Leadership	○ ↑	○ ↑	⊙ ↑	⊙ ↑	■	4	0	24

Relationship Strength

⊙ = 9 Significant
○ = 3 Medium
△ = 1 Weak

Information provided courtesy of U.S. Air Force, Air Combat Command

Interrelationship Digraph

Issues Surrounding Implementation of the Business Plan

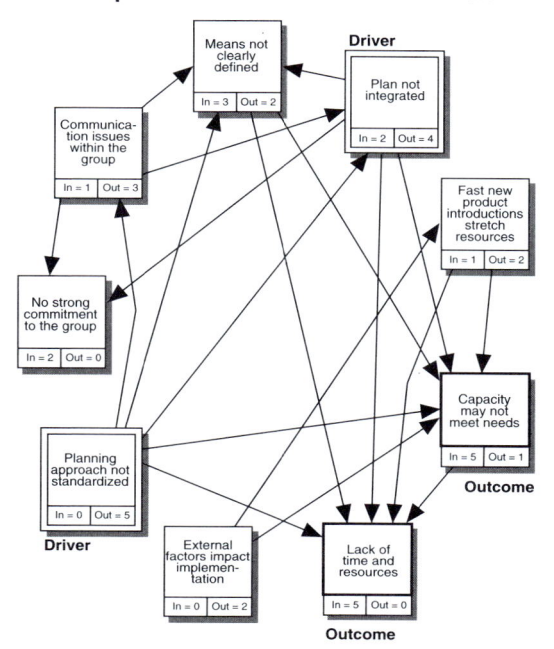

Means not clearly defined
In = 3 | Out = 2

Plan not integrated — Driver
In = 2 | Out = 4

Communication issues within the group
In = 1 | Out = 3

Fast new product introductions stretch resources
In = 1 | Out = 2

No strong commitment to the group
In = 2 | Out = 0

Planning approach not standardized — Driver
In = 0 | Out = 5

External factors impact implementation
In = 0 | Out = 2

Capacity may not meet needs — Outcome
In = 5 | Out = 1

Lack of time and resources — Outcome
In = 5 | Out = 0

Information provided courtesy of Goodyear

Note: The "drivers" from this ID will be used as the goal in the Tree example shown at the end of the Tree Diagram/PDPC section.

Interrelationship Digraph

A Vision of Andover in the 21st Century

See next page for close-up

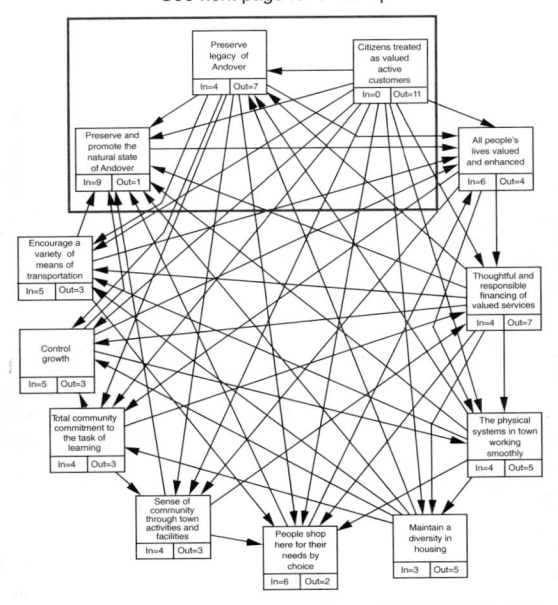

- Preserve legacy of Andover — In=4, Out=7
- Citizens treated as valued active customers — In=0, Out=11
- Preserve and promote the natural state of Andover — In=9, Out=1
- All people's lives valued and enhanced — In=6, Out=4
- Encourage a variety of means of transportation — In=5, Out=3
- Thoughtful and responsible financing of valued services — In=4, Out=7
- Control growth — In=5, Out=3
- Total community commitment to the task of learning — In=4, Out=3
- The physical systems in town working smoothly — In=4, Out=5
- Sense of community through town activities and facilities — In=4, Out=3
- People shop here for their needs by choice — In=6, Out=2
- Maintain a diversity in housing — In=3, Out=5

Information provided courtesy of Town of Andover, MA

154 Interrelationship Digraph ©2002 GOAL/QPC

Interrelationship Digraph

A Vision of Andover in the 21st Century

Close-up

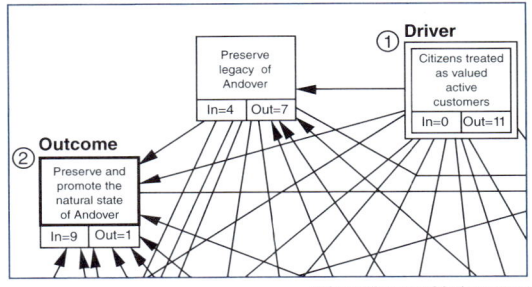

```
                    Preserve              ① Driver
                    legacy of           Citizens treated
                    Andover              as valued
                   ┌─────────┐            active
                   │In=4 Out=7│          customers
                                        ┌──────────┐
  ② Outcome                             │In=0 Out=11│
   Preserve and
   promote the
   natural state
   of Andover
  ┌─────────┐
  │In=9 Out=1│
```

Information provided courtesy of Town of Andover, MA

① This is the driver. If the focus on the citizen as a customer becomes the core of the town's vision, then everything else will be advanced.

② This is the primary outcome. It puts the preservation of nature in the town as a key indicator of the vision working.

©2002 GOAL/QPC

Involvement Matrix
Involving people in your project

Why use it?
To determine the appropriate level of involvement for different groups of stakeholders.

What does it do?
- Identifies the many people involved in making a change happen
- Describes the level of involvement required of each stakeholder group. Not everyone needs to be completely involved at every stage.
- Maps the involvement required for the major tasks in the project

The matrix on the next page will help you think about who should be involved in the different steps needed to make change a reality, as well as what level of involvement is appropriate for them.

A Sample Involvement Matrix

Task	Which groups or individuals should be:			
	Responsible for	Involved in	Consulted with regarding	Informed about
Identifying solutions				
Selecting solutions				
Planning the implementation				
Handling potential problems				
Implementing the solution				
Monitoring results				

Tip Developing, implementing, and monitoring solutions are most often group tasks. People involved in implementation or monitoring will have more commitment to a solution if they are also involved in its development.

Kano Model
Categorizing customer needs

Why use it?
To identify and prioritize the full range of your customers' needs.

What does it do?
- Helps to describe which needs, if fulfilled, contribute to customer dissatisfaction, neutrality, or delight

- Identifies the "Must Be" needs, which are those that the customer expects. If they are unfulfilled, the customer is dissatisfied; however, even if they are completely fulfilled, the customer is not particularly satisfied. An example of a Must Be need is airline safety.

- Identifies the "More Is Better" needs, which are those that have a linear effect on customer satisfaction: The more these needs are met, the more satisfied customers are. An example is inexpensive airline tickets.

- Identifies "Delighter" needs, which are those that do not cause dissatisfaction when not present but satisfy the customer when they are. An example is serving hot chocolate chip cookies during an airline flight.

- Assists in the prioritization of needs—for example, Must Be needs are generally taken for granted unless they are absent. Take care of these needs first.

The Kano Model

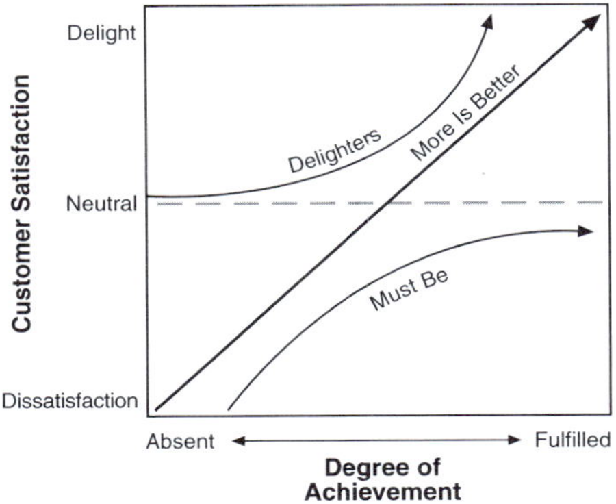
Delight
Customer Satisfaction
Neutral
Dissatisfaction
Delighters
More Is Better
Must Be
Absent
Fulfilled
Degree of Achievement

How do I do it?

1. Gather sorted customer needs from the Customer-Data Affinity Diagram. (See the CTQ Tree section for details.)

Customer-Data Affinity Diagram

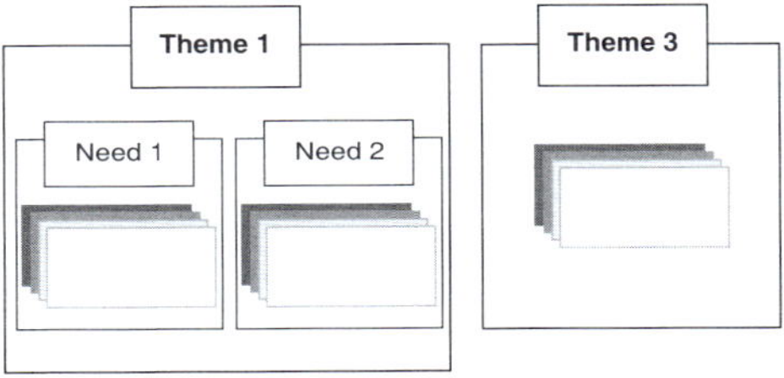
Theme 1
Need 1
Need 2
Theme 3

2. **Review the themes from the Affinity Diagram and sort them into the three categories in the Kano Model (Must Be, More Is Better, and Delighters)**

3. **If there are very few or no needs listed in one of the categories, collect additional customer data**

    Tip Customers generally cannot articulate what their basic expectations are or what would delight them. Therefore, when you prioritize customer needs based on what they say is important, you must remember that generally they will identify only More Is Better characteristics. You must use other means—such as direct observation of customer use—to identify and set priorities for Must Be characteristics and Delighters.

4. **After you have collected additional data, return to the Kano categories and complete the sorting of customer needs**

5. **Prioritize the customer needs you will use when you develop CTQs (see the CTQ Tree section for details)**

    Tip First work on any Must Be characteristics that, if absent, would create customer dissatisfaction. Consider the importance of More Is Better characteristics to provide steady and strong increases in satisfaction, and include in your priorities a few Delighters that will increase satisfaction dramatically. Also consider how these categories relate to your company's competitive advantage.

Customer Expectations for a Hotel Room

	Must Be	**More Is Better**	**Delighters**
Hotel Room	• Bed • Clean towels • Phone • Coffee maker	• Number/thickness of towels • Size of room	• Fruit basket upon arrival • Balcony • Free movies

Tip Customer needs change over time. A Delighter today might be a Must Be tomorrow. In addition, different customer segments might have different needs. For example, a business traveler might consider a hotel-room iron a Must Be and the size of the desk's work surface a More Is Better. A family traveling on vacation, on the other hand, might consider free movies and video games a More Is Better characteristic.

Matrix Diagram
Finding relationships

Why use it?

To allow a team or individual to systematically identify, analyze, and rate the presence and strength of relationships between two or more sets of information.

What does it do?

- Makes patterns of responsibilities visible and clear so that there is an even and appropriate distribution of tasks
- Helps a team get consensus on small decisions, enhancing the quality and support for the final decision
- Improves a team's discipline in systematically taking a hard look at a large number of important decision factors

Types of Matrices

Most Common

- *L-shaped matrix.* Two sets of items directly compared to each other, or a single set compared to itself.

Orienting New Employees

Tasks / Resources	Tour facility	Review personnel & safety policies	Review business values	Introduce to team members
Human resources		○	△	
Division manager			●	
Supervisor	△	●	○	○
Associates	●	△	△	●

● Primary responsibility
○ Team members
△ Resources

Conclusion: Supervisors and associates have taken on the orientation role rather than the traditional human resource function.

- *T-shaped matrix.* Two sets of items compared to a common third set.

Orienting New Employees

Communicate organization spirit	●	○	●	●
Communicate purpose of organization			●	●
Resolve practical concerns	●	●	○	●
Reduce anxiety	●	●	●	●
Goals / Resources \ Tasks	Tour facility	Review personnel & safety policies	Review business values	Introduce to team members
Human resources		○		△
Division manager			●	
Supervisor	△	●	○	○
Associates	●	△	△	●

Responsibility
● Primary
○ Team members
△ Resources

Impact
● High
○ Medium
△ Low

Conclusion: The most important purpose of orientation is to reduce anxiety, and the most effective tasks focus on the personal issues.

Uncommon

- *Y-shaped matrix.* Three sets of items compared to each other. It "bends" a T-shaped matrix to allow comparisons between items that are on the vertical axes.

Rarely Used

- *X-shaped matrix.* Four sets of items compared to each other. It is essentially two T-shaped matrices placed back to back.

- *C-shaped matrix.* Shows the intersection of three sets of data simultaneously. It is a three-dimensional graphic.
- You can find more complete information on the Y-, X-, and C-shaped matrix in *The Memory Jogger Plus+®*.

How do I do it?

1. **Select the key factors affecting successful implementation**
   - The most important step is to choose the issues or factors to be compared. The format is secondary. Begin with the right issues, and the best format will define itself. The most common use is the distribution of responsibilities within an L-shaped or T-shaped matrix.

2. **Assemble the right team**
   - Select individuals that have the influence/power to realistically assess the chosen factors.

   Tip When distributing responsibilities, include those people who will likely be involved in the assigned tasks or who can at least be part of a review team to confirm small-group results.

3. **Select an appropriate matrix format**
   - Base your choice of format on the number of sets of items and types of comparisons you need to make.

4. **Choose and define relationship symbols**
   - The most common symbols in matrix analysis are ⊙, ○, and △. Generally they are used to indicate:

     ⊙ = High   = 9
     ○ = Medium = 3
     △ = Low   = 1

- The possible meanings of the symbols are almost endless. The only requirement is that the team comes to a clear understanding and creates an equally clear legend with the matrix.

5. **Complete the matrix**
    - If distributing responsibilities, use only one "primary responsibility" symbol to show ultimate accountability. All other core team members can be given secondary responsibilities.

    Tip Focus the quality of the decision in each matrix cell. Do not try to "stack the deck" by consciously building a pattern of decisions. Let these patterns emerge naturally.

    Tip Interpret the matrix using total numerical values only when it adds value. Often the visual pattern is sufficient to interpret the overall results.

Variations

The matrix is one of the most versatile tools available. The important skill to master is "matrix thinking." This approach allows a team to focus its discussion on related factors that are explored thoroughly. The separate conclusions are then brought together to create high-quality decisions. Use your creativity in determining which factors affect each other and in choosing the matrix format that will help focus the discussion toward the ultimate decision.

Matrix
Logistics Annual Plan

Information provided courtesy of Bell Canada

Goal: Continue to implement total quality → Delight our customers

TQ Implementation (Tree):
- Survey customer satisfaction
- Research customer needs via QFD
- Capture customer comments

LQC Objectives (Matrix):
- Reduce customer cost
- Continue implementation of total quality
- Continue upgrading tech., prof., & managerial skills of employees
- Promote environmental responsibility in our operations

Measures:
- % satisfaction via survey
- List of customer needs by key processes
- # of comments or # of complaints

TQ Implementation	Reduce customer cost	Continue implementation of total quality	Continue upgrading skills	Promote environmental responsibility	Measures	2003 Quarter 1 2 3 4	2004 Quarter 1 2 3 4
Survey customer satisfaction	△	⊙		○	% satisfaction via survey	▲	See next page ①
Research customer needs via QFD	△	⊙	△	○	List of customer needs by key processes		▲
Capture customer comments	○	⊙	△	△	# of comments or # of complaints	▲	

- ⊙ = 9 Strong influence/relationship
- ○ = 3 Some influence/relationship
- △ = 1 Weak influence/relationship
- Blank = No influence/relationship

166 Matrix Diagram ©2002 GOAL/QPC

Matrix

Logistics Annual Plan (cont.)

TQ Implementation (Tree)		Goals (AND)		Co-Responsibility (Matrix)					Cost/Benefit Analysis				Status*
		2003	2004	LOC	Departments	Boards of management	Logistical	Other stakeholders	Resources required ($) 03	04	Tangible benefits ($) 03	04	
Goal: Continue to implement total quality	Delight our customers	Survey customer satisfaction	75% customer satisfaction	80% customer satisfaction	◉	○	○	○	△	25K	25K			
		Research customer needs via QFD	Field trial	100% customer needs gathered	△	◉	△	◉	△	25K	25K			
		Capture customer comments	1% transactions	1.9%	△	◉	○	○	△					

① from previous page

◉ = 9 Prime responsibility
○ = 3 Secondary responsibility
△ = 1 Kept informed

*Status: ▨ Caution ■ Stopped ☐ On target

Information provided courtesy of Bell Canada

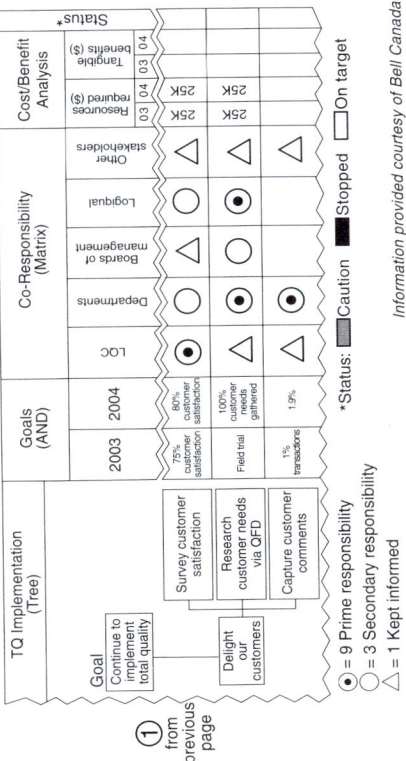

©2002 GOAL/QPC Matrix Diagram 167

Measurement Systems Analysis (MSA)
Understanding measurement variation

Why use it?

Measurement Systems Analysis (MSA) is a type of experiment where you measure the same item repeatedly using different people or pieces of equipment. MSA is used to quantify the amount of variation in a measure that comes from the measurement system itself rather than from product or process variation. It is most commonly used in the Measure step of the DMAIC method to assess whether you need to improve your measurement system before you collect data.

What does it do?

- Helps you to determine how much of an observed variation is due to the measurement system itself
- Helps you to determine the ways in which a measurement system needs to be improved
- Assesses a measurement system for some or all of the following five characteristics:

  ### 1. Accuracy

  Accuracy is attained when the measured value has little deviation from the actual value. Accuracy is usually tested by comparing an average of repeated measurements to a known standard value for that unit of measure.

Determining Accuracy

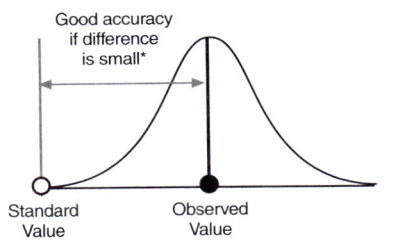

Good accuracy if difference is small*

Standard Value — Observed Value

2. Repeatability

Repeatability is attained when the same person taking multiple measurements on the same item or characteristic gets the same result every time.

Determining Repeatability

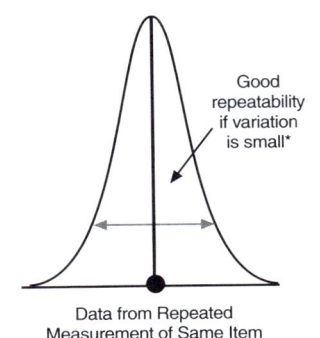

Good repeatability if variation is small*

Data from Repeated Measurement of Same Item

©2002 GOAL/QPC **Measurement Systems Analysis** 169

3. Reproducibility

Reproducibility is attained when other people (or other instruments or labs) get the same results you get when measuring the same item or characteristic.

Determining Reproducibility

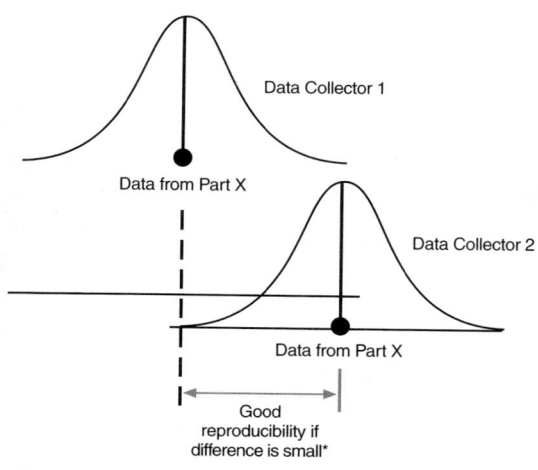

Data Collector 1

Data from Part X

Data Collector 2

Data from Part X

Good reproducibility if difference is small*

*Small relative to a) product variation and b) product tolerance (the width of the product specifications)

4. Stability

Stability is attained when measurements that are taken by one person in the same way vary little over time.

Determining Stability

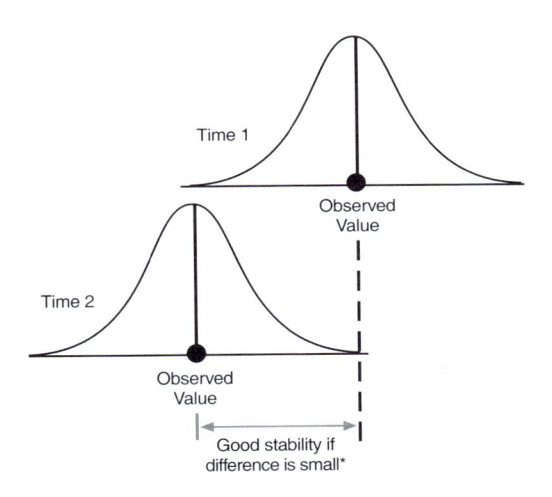

Time 1 — Observed Value

Time 2 — Observed Value

Good stability if difference is small*

5. Adequate Resolution

Adequate resolution means that your measurement instrument can give at least five (and preferably more) distinct values in the range you need to measure. For example, if you measure the heights of adults with a device that measures only to the nearest foot, you will get readings of just three distinct values: four feet, five feet, and six feet. If you needed to measure lengths between 5.1 centimeters and 5.5 centimeters, to get adequate resolution the measurement instrument you used would have to be capable of measuring to the nearest 0.1 centimeter to give five distinct values in the measurement range, as shown in the graph on the next page.

Determining Adequate Resolution

```
                    X
                    X
           X        X
           X        X        X
           X        X        X        X
   X       X        X        X        X
  5.1     5.2      5.3      5.4      5.5
```

How do I do it?

1. Conduct an experiment where different people (or machines) measure the same group of items repeatedly. This group should contain items that vary enough to cover the full range of typical variation.

Measurements by Unit Number and Operator

Unit #	Operator	Measurement	Unit #	Operator	Measurement
1	Joe	11.34	3	Sally	12.18
1	Joe	11.29	3	Sally	12.23
1	Joe	11.33	3	Sally	12.14
1	Joe	11.24	3	Sally	12.17
1	Sally	11.19	4	Joe	13.27
1	Sally	11.29	4	Joe	13.28
1	Sally	11.21	4	Joe	13.24
1	Sally	11.24	4	Joe	13.23
2	Joe	11.65	4	Sally	13.09
2	Joe	11.60	4	Sally	13.14
2	Joe	11.67	4	Sally	13.02
2	Joe	11.56	4	Sally	13.19
2	Sally	11.50	5	Joe	11.84
2	Sally	11.55	5	Joe	11.89
2	Sally	11.51	5	Joe	11.93
2	Sally	11.55	5	Joe	11.85
3	Joe	12.31	5	Sally	11.76
3	Joe	12.28	5	Sally	11.84
3	Joe	12.31	5	Sally	11.81
3	Joe	12.34	5	Sally	11.78

Here, two people each measured five units four times.

2. Plot the data.

A Run Chart of the Measurements

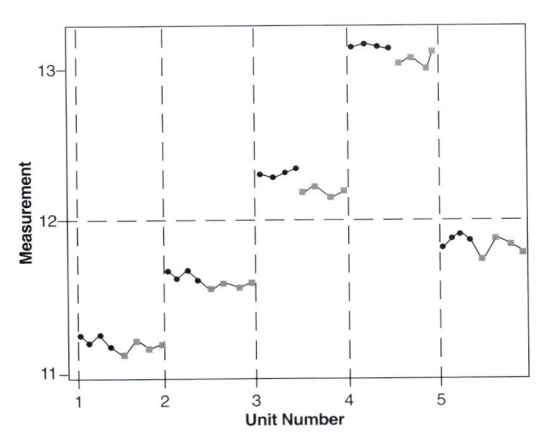

- Joe
- Sally

Very little difference is seen in repeated measurements done by the same person or by different people.

3. Analyze the data. Use statistical techniques such as Analysis of Variance (ANOVA) to determine what portion of the variation is due to operator differences and what portion is due to the measurement process.

4. Improve the measurement process, if necessary. Do this based on what you learn from your analysis. For example, if there is too much person-to-person variation, your measurement method must be standardized for multiple persons.

The examples shown on the previous pages pertain to continuous measurement systems. A similar approach can be used for discrete measurement systems, in which items are categorized (e.g., good/bad; type of call received; reason for leaving). In these cases, you need to have a high degree of agreement on the way an item should be categorized. The best way to assess this is to have all your operators repeatedly categorize several "known" test units. Ideally, all your operators will arrive at 100% agreement: Each operator matches his or her own previous assessments, those of the other operators, and the "correct" assessments. Use any disagreements that arise as opportunities to determine and eliminate problems with your measurement system.

For example, help-desk associates might categorize incoming calls by call type. One way to test this measurement system is to have an expert categorize 100 recorded calls and then play each of the recordings twice, in random order, to four different associates. You can then document the associates' categorizations along with the expert's categorizations and analyze them for discrepancies.

Tip When doing MSA, you learn how much variation the measurement system itself contributes. Here are some guidelines for determining if that variation is too great. For continuous measurement systems, the standard deviation for the operator and measurement instrument combined should be no more than one-third the observed total standard deviation of the product. (This is derived from measuring several products and determining the standard deviation from them.) In addition, this measurement standard deviation should be no more than one-eighteenth of the specified desired product performance. For example, if the process is supposed to give results of between 5.0 and 5.18, the total measurement standard deviation should be no more than .01 (i.e., (5.18 − 5.0) ÷ 18).

No such guidelines exist for discrete measurement systems. You should investigate each measurement discrepancy (i.e., one measurer classifies an object as x, and another measurer classifies it as y) and change the process to remove the discrepancy in the future if possible.

Tip Because MSA can be quite complex, generally Six Sigma Experts or Master Six Sigma Experts are involved in the design and analysis of these experiments.

Variation

Sometimes MSA is called Gauge R&R; the *R&R* stands for Repeatability and Reproducibility.

Operational Definitions
Removing ambiguity in data collection

Why use it?
To define, for each measurement, what the key characteristic is and how to measure it.

What does it do?
- Provides a precise description for data collectors
- Removes ambiguity so that all people involved have the same understanding of the characteristic in question
- Tells how to get a value for the characteristic you are trying to measure
- Describes your way of measuring that characteristic

How do I do it?

1. **Develop a draft definition. Include what the characteristic is and how to measure it.**

    - You must be able to count defects to calculate the process sigma. In some cases, it's obvious what a defect is; in other cases, you must create a definition.

    - The definition must be specific and concrete so that different people can use it and know that their data will all be measured in the same way.

    - The definition must be measurable. This means you can assign a value (either a number or yes/no) to a data point.

    - The definition must be useful to both you and your customers. To be useful, it should relate to how the customers will judge quality and should allow a go/

no-go decision—"yes, we've met the customers' need" or "no, we haven't met the customers' need."

2. **Test the definition on a small sample of data**

3. **Modify the definition as necessary**

   Tip There is no single right way to define a measure. But all your data collectors must agree on the definition you use. The more specific you are, the better.

   Tip Training will help data collectors consistently apply your definition.

Examples

Operational definition for defect-free animal crackers

- A defect-free animal cracker is one with the animal completely intact. The entire body of the animal should be whole, and there should be no additional pieces of cracker (spurs, etc.) beyond the edges of the animal except for background pieces that are intended to be part of the cracker. There should be no additional gaps or holes in the animal's background.

- The embossed pattern of the animal should be clear for the entire cracker from a distance of four feet.

- The color of a defect-free animal cracker should be no lighter than the lightest cracker in the sample and no darker than the darkest cracker in the sample.

Operational definition for teller service at a bank

Customers' waiting time in line at the bank is measured, in minutes and seconds, from the point at which the customer steps behind the last person in the line to the point at which the teller greets him/her. Any wait time longer than four minutes is considered a defect.

Pareto Chart
Focus on key problems

Why use it?
To focus efforts on the problems that offer the greatest potential for improvement by showing their relative frequency or size in a descending bar graph.

What does it do?
- Helps a team to focus on those causes that will have the greatest impact if solved
- Based on the proven Pareto principle: 20% of the sources cause 80% of any problem
- Displays the relative importance of problems in a simple, quickly interpreted, visual format
- Helps prevent "shifting the problem" where the "solution" removes some causes but worsens others
- Progress is measured in a highly visible format that provides incentive to push on for more improvement

How do I do it?

1. **Decide which problem you want to know more about**

   Example: Consider the case of HOTrep, an internal computer network help line: Why do people call the HOTrep help line; what problems are people having?

2. **Choose the causes or problems that will be monitored, compared, and rank ordered by brainstorming or with existing data**

   a) Brainstorming

   Example: What are typical problems that users ask about on the HOTrep help line?

b) Based on existing data

> **Example:** What problems in the last month have users called about on the HOTrep help line?

3. Choose the most meaningful unit of measurement, such as frequency or cost

- Sometimes you don't know before the study which unit of measurement is best. Be prepared to do both frequency and cost.

   Example: For the HOTrep data the most important measure is frequency because the project team can use the information to simplify software, improve documentation or training, or solve bigger system problems.

4. Choose the time period for the study

- Choose a time period that is long enough to represent the situation. Longer studies don't always translate to *better* information. Look first at volume and variety within the data.
- Make sure the scheduled time is typical in order to take into account seasonality or even different patterns within a given day or week.

   Example: Review HOTrep help line calls for 10 weeks (May 22–August 4).

5. Gather the necessary data on each problem category either by "real time" or reviewing historical data

- Whether data is gathered in "real time" or historically, check sheets are the easiest method for collecting data.

   Example: Gathered HOTrep help line calls data based on the review of incident reports (historical).

   Tip *Always* include with the source data and the final chart the identifiers that indicate the source, location, and time period covered.

6. **Compare the relative frequency or cost of each problem category**

   Example:

Problem Category	Frequency	Percent (%)
Bad configuration	3	1
Boot problems	68	33
File problems	8	4
Lat. connection	20	10
Print problems	16	8
Reflection hang	24	12
Reflection sys. integrity	11	5
Reflections misc.	6	3
System configuration	16	8
System integrity	19	9
Others	15	7
Total	206	

7. **List the problem categories on the horizontal line and frequencies on the vertical line**

   - List the categories in descending order from left to right on the horizontal line with bars above each problem category to indicate its frequency or cost. List the unit of measure on the vertical line.

8. **(Optional) Draw the cumulative percentage line showing the portion of the total that each problem category represents**

   a) On the vertical line, (opposite the raw data, #, $, etc.), record 100% opposite the total number and 50% at the halfway point. Fill in the remaining percentages drawn to scale.

   b) Starting with the highest problem category, put a dot or an x at the upper righthand corner of the bar.

   - Add the total of the next problem category to the first and draw a dot above that bar showing both the cumulative number and percentage. Connect the dots and record the remaining cumulative totals until 100% is reached.

HOTrep Problem Data

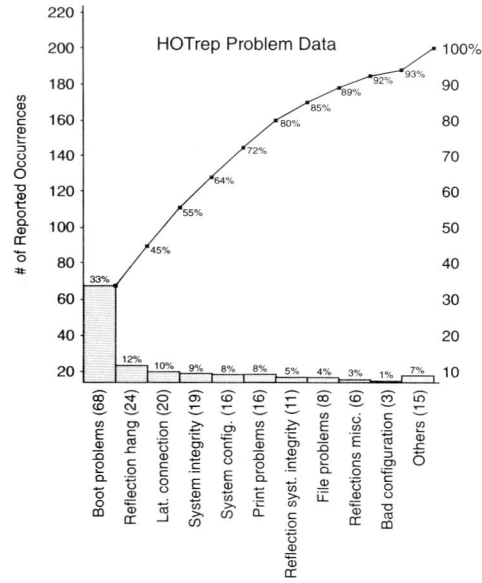

Chart data (bars, # of Reported Occurrences):
- Boot problems (68) — 33%
- Reflection hang (24) — 12%
- Lat. connection (20) — 10%
- System integrity (19) — 9%
- System config. (16) — 8%
- Print problems (16) — 8%
- Reflection syst. integrity (11) — 5%
- File problems (8) — 4%
- Reflections misc. (6) — 3%
- Bad configuration (3) — 1%
- Others (15) — 7%

Cumulative %: 33, 45, 55, 64, 72, 80, 85, 89, 92, 93, 100

Information provided courtesy of SmithKline Beecham

9. Interpret the results

- *Generally*, the tallest bars indicate the biggest contributors to the overall problem. Dealing with these problem categories first therefore makes common sense. *But*, the most frequent or expensive is not always the most important. Always ask: What has the most impact on the goals of our business and customers?

Variations

The Pareto Chart is one of the most widely and creatively used improvement tools. The variations used most frequently are listed below. Examples are shown on pages 184–188.

A. Major Cause Breakdowns in which the "tallest bar" is broken into subcauses in a second, linked Pareto.

B. Before and After in which the "new Pareto" bars are drawn side by side with the original Pareto, showing the effect of a change. It can be drawn as one chart or two separate charts.

C. Change the Source of Data in which data is collected on the same problem but from different departments, locations, equipment, and so on, and shown in side-by-side Pareto Charts.

D. Change Measurement Scale in which the same categories are used but measured differently. Typically "cost" and "frequency" are alternated.

Pareto Chart Stratification

As described in the Data Collection section, stratification can provide useful insight into what is actually happening in your process. Some Pareto Charts can be stratified.

Example

The team at XYZ Company decided to focus on errors made on faxed orders, since more errors occurred with those orders than with e-mail or web orders. To get an idea of the types of errors that occurred, the team randomly selected 400 orders from a group of 4000+ orders and catalogued the types of errors encountered. They counted almost 900 errors made on the 400 orders. They plotted their data in three different ways, as shown in the Pareto Charts on the next page.

Errors Made on 400 Orders

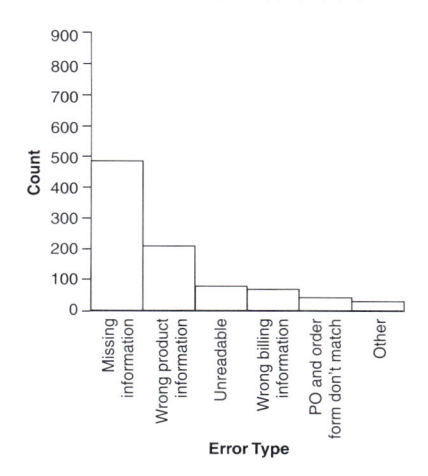

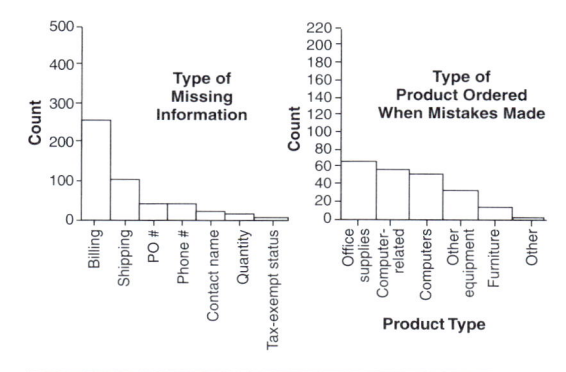

Type of Missing Information

Type of Product Ordered When Mistakes Made

Pareto 183

Pareto

A. Major Cause Breakdowns

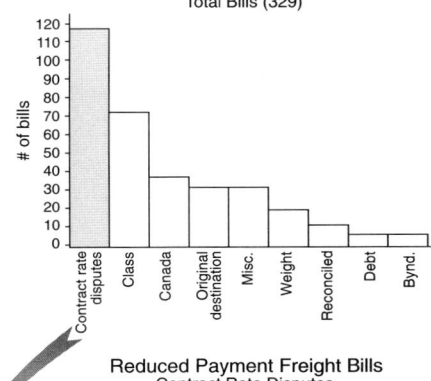

Reduced Payment Freight Bills
Total Bills (329)

Bar chart — # of bills:
- Contract rate disputes: ~118
- Class: ~72
- Canada: ~37
- Original destination: ~32
- Misc.: ~31
- Weight: ~20
- Reconciled: ~12
- Debt: ~7
- Bynd.: ~5

Reduced Payment Freight Bills
Contract Rate Disputes

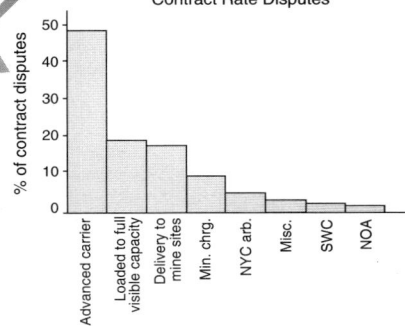

Bar chart — % of contract disputes:
- Advanced carrier: ~49
- Loaded to full visible capacity: ~19
- Delivery to mine sites: ~17
- Min. chrg.: ~9
- NYC arb.: ~5
- Misc.: ~3
- SWC: ~2
- NOA: ~1

Information provided courtesy of Goodyear

184 Pareto

©2002 GOAL/QPC

Pareto
B. Before and After

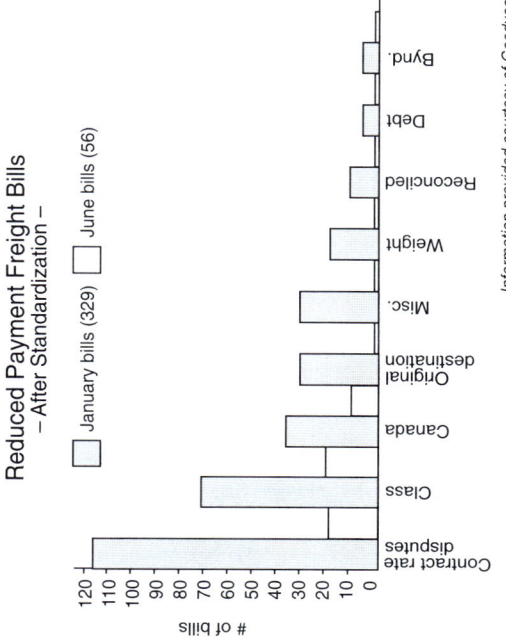

Reduced Payment Freight Bills
— After Standardization —

Legend: January bills (329), June bills (56)

Categories (# of bills): Contract rate disputes, Class, Canada, Original destination, Misc., Weight, Reconciled, Debt, Bynd.

Information provided courtesy of Goodyear

Pareto
C. Change the Source of Data

Reason for Failed Appointments
Source of Data is: Shore Commands

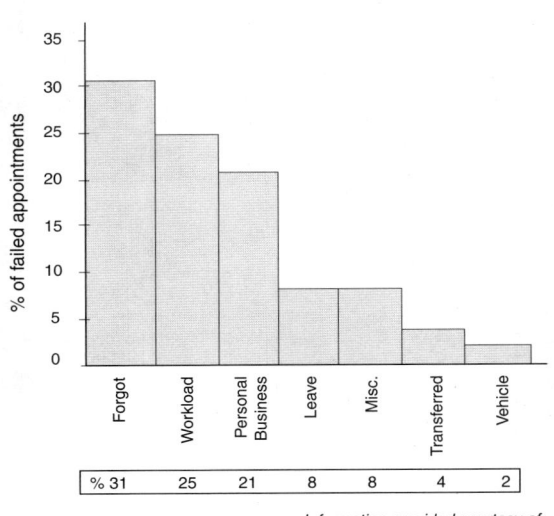

	Forgot	Workload	Personal Business	Leave	Misc.	Transferred	Vehicle
%	31	25	21	8	8	4	2

*Information provided courtesy of
U.S. Navy, Naval Dental Center, San Diego*

Pareto

C. Change the Source of Data

Reason for Failed Appointments
Source of Data is: Fleet Commands

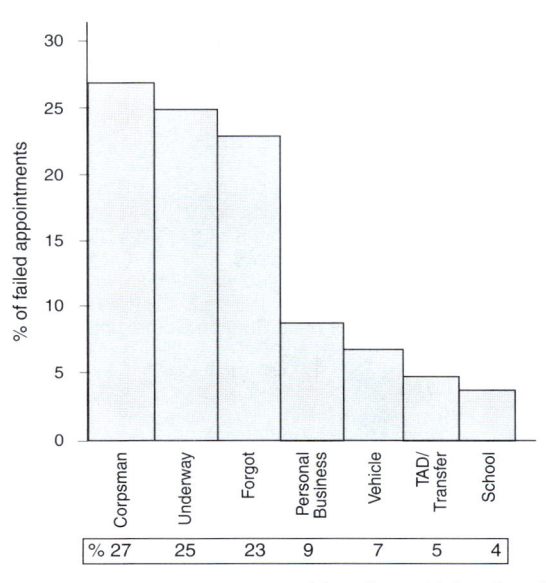

	Corpsman	Underway	Forgot	Personal Business	Vehicle	TAD/Transfer	School
%	27	25	23	9	7	5	4

*Information provided courtesy of
U.S. Navy, Naval Dental Center, San Diego*

D. Change Measurement Scale

Field Service Customer Complaints

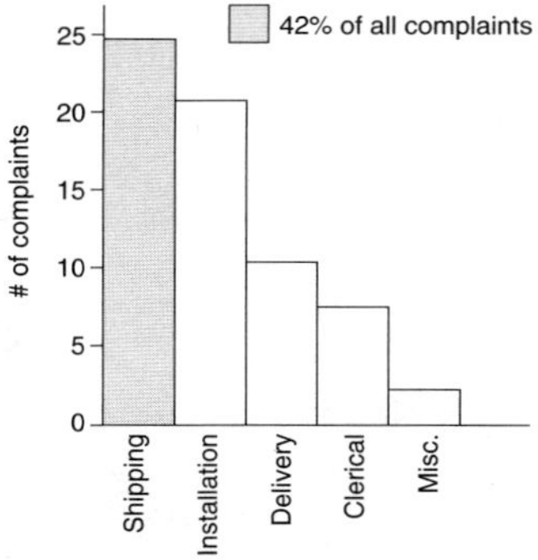
42% of all complaints
# of complaints
25
20
15
10
5
0
Shipping
Installation
Delivery
Clerical
Misc.

Cost to Rectify Field Service Complaints

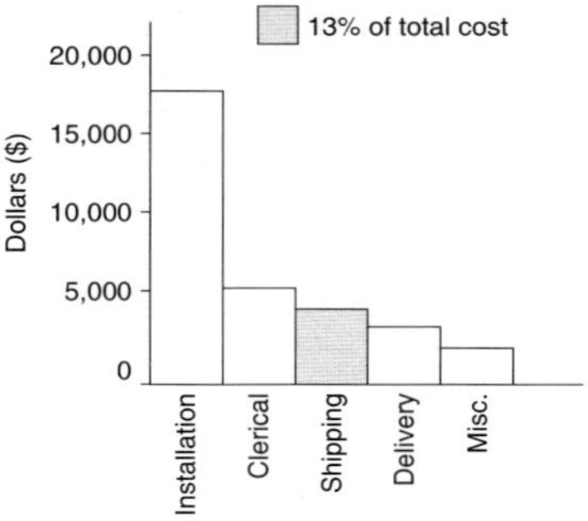
13% of total cost
Dollars ($)
20,000
15,000
10,000
5,000
0
Installation
Clerical
Shipping
Delivery
Misc.

Prioritization Matrices
Weighing your options

Why use it?
To narrow down options through a systematic approach of comparing choices by selecting, weighting, and applying criteria.

What does it do?
- Quickly surfaces basic disagreements so they may be resolved up front
- Forces a team to focus on the best thing(s) to do, and not everything they could do, dramatically increasing the chances for implementation success
- Limits "hidden agendas" by surfacing the criteria as a necessary part of the process
- Increases the chance of follow-through because consensus is sought at each step in the process (from criteria to conclusions)
- Reduces the chances of selecting someone's "pet project"

How do I do it?
There are three methods for constructing Prioritization Matrices. The outline that follows indicates typical situations for using each method. Only the "Full Analytical Criteria Method" is discussed here. The others are covered fully in *The Memory Jogger Plus+®*.

Full Analytical Criteria Method

Typically used when:
- Smaller teams are involved (3–8 people).
- Options are few (5–10 choices).
- There are relatively few criteria (3–6 items).
- Complete consensus is needed.
- The stakes are high if the plan fails.

Consensus Criteria Method

This method follows the same steps as in the Full Analytical Criteria Method except the Consensus Criteria Method uses a combination of weighted voting, and ranking is used instead of paired comparisons.

Typically used when:
- Larger teams are involved (8 or more people).
- Options are many (10–20 choices).
- There is a significant number of criteria (6–15 items).
- Quick consensus is needed to proceed.

Combination ID/Matrix Method

This method is different from the other two methods because it is based on cause and effect, rather than criteria.

Typically used when:
- Interrelationships among options are high, and finding the option with the greatest impact is critical.

Full Analytical Criteria Method

1. **Agree on the ultimate goal to be achieved in a clear, concise sentence**
   - If no other tools are used as input, produce a clear goal statement through consensus. This statement strongly affects which criteria are used.

   > Choose the most enjoyable vacation for the whole family

2. **Create the list of criteria**
   - Brainstorm the list of criteria or review previous documents or guidelines that are available, e.g., corporate goals, budget-related guidelines.

   > - Cost
   > - Educational value
   > - Diverse activity
   > - Escape reality

   Tip The team *must reach consensus* on the final criteria and their meanings, or the process is likely to fail!

3. **Using an L-shaped matrix, weight all criteria against each other**
   - Reading across from the vertical axis, compare each criterion to those on the horizontal axis.
   - Each time a weight (e.g., 1, 5, 10) is recorded in a row cell, its reciprocal value (e.g., $1/5$, $1/10$) must be recorded in the corresponding column cell.
   - Total each horizontal row and convert to a relative decimal value known as the "criteria weighting."

Criterion vs. Criterion

Criteria \ Criteria	Cost	Educ. value	Diverse activity	Escape reality	Row Total	Relative Decimal Value
Cost		$\frac{1}{5}$	$\frac{1}{10}$	5	5.3	.15
Educ. value	5		$\frac{1}{5}$	5	10.2	.28
Diverse activity	10	5		5	20	.55
Escape reality	$\frac{1}{5}$	$\frac{1}{5}$	$\frac{1}{5}$		.60	.02
				Grand Total	36.1	

1 = Equally important
5 = More important
10 = Much more important
$1/5$ = Less Important
$1/10$ = Much less important

Row Total
Rating scores added
Grand Total
Row totals added
Relative Decimal Value
Each row total ÷ by the grand total

4. **Compare ALL options relative to each weighted criterion**
   - *For each criterion*, create an L-shaped matrix with all of the options on both the vertical and horizontal axis and the criteria listed in the lefthand corner of the matrix. *There will be as many options matrices as there are criteria to be applied.*
   - Use the same rating scale (1, 5, 10) as in Step 3, *BUT* customize the wording for each criterion.
   - The relative decimal value is the "option rating."

---

192 Prioritization Matrices

Options vs. Each Criterion (Cost Criterion)

Cost	Disney World	Gettysburg	New York City	Uncle Henry's	Row Total	Relative Decimal Value
Disney World		$\frac{1}{5}$	5	$\frac{1}{10}$	5.3	.12
Gettysburg	5		10	$\frac{1}{5}$	15.2	.33
New York City	$\frac{1}{5}$	$\frac{1}{10}$		$\frac{1}{10}$	.40	.01
Uncle Henry's	10	5	10		25	.54
				Grand Total	45.9	

1 = Equal cost
5 = Less expensive
10 = Much less expensive
$1/5$ = More expensive
$1/10$ = Much more expensive

Continue Step 4 through three more Options/Criterion matrices, like this:

Escape reality

Crt.	Options		
Options			

Diverse activity

Crt.	Options		
Options			

Educational value

Crt.	Options		
Options			

Tip The whole number (1, 5, 10) must always represent a desirable rating. In some cases this may mean "less," e.g., cost; in others this may mean "more," e.g., tasty.

5. **Using an L-shaped summary matrix, compare each option based on all criteria combined**
   - List all criteria on the horizontal axis and all options on the vertical axis.
   - In each matrix cell multiply the "criteria weighting" of each criterion (decimal value from Step 3) by the "option rating" (decimal value from Step 4). This creates an "option score."
   - Add each option score across all criteria for a row total. Divide each row total by the grand total and convert to the final decimal value. Compare these decimal values to help you decide which option to pursue.

Summary Matrix
Options vs. All Criteria

Criteria \ Optns.	Cost (.15)	Educational value (.28)	Diverse activity (.55)	Escape reality (.02)	Row Total	Relative Decimal Value (RT ÷ GT)
Disney World	.12 x .15 (.02)	.24 x .28 (.07)	.40 x .55 (.22)	.65 x .02 (.01)	.32	.32
Gettysburg	.33 x .15 (.05)	.37 x .28 (.10)	.10 x .55 (.06)	.22 x .02 (0)	.22	.22
New York City	.01 x .15 (0)	.37 x .28 (.10)	.49 x .55 (.27)	.12 x .02 (0)	.37	.38
Uncle Henry's	.54 x .15 (.08)	.01 x .28 (0)	.01 x .55 (.01)	.01 x .02 (0)	.09	.09
				Grand Total	1.00	

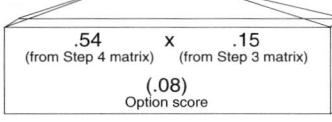

.54   x   .15
(from Step 4 matrix)   (from Step 3 matrix)

(.08)
Option score

194 Prioritization Matrices

6. **Choose the best option(s) across all criteria**

    Tip While this is more systematic than traditional decision making, it is not a science. Use common sense and judgment when options are rated very closely, but be open to non-traditional conclusions as well.

Variations

See *The Memory Jogger Plus+*® for full explanations of both the Consensus Criteria Method and the Combination ID/Matrix Method. The Full Analytical Criteria Method, illustrated in this book, is recommended because it encourages full discussion and consensus on critical issues. The Full Analytical Criteria Method is a simplified adaptation of an even more rigorous model known as the Analytical Hierarchy Process. It is based on the work of Thomas Saaty, which he describes in his book *Decision Making for Leaders*. In any case, use common sense to know when a situation is important enough to warrant such thorough processes.

Another type of matrix your team can use to select the best and strongest idea or concept from dozens or hundreds of possibilities is Stuart Pugh's New Concept Selection tool. For details, see pages 193 through 206 of *The Idea Edge*™.

Prioritization
Choosing a Standard Corporate Spreadsheet Program

① Weighting criteria (described in Step 3)

This is a portion of a full matrix with 14 criteria in total.

Criteria	Best use of hardware	Ease of use	Maximum functionality	Best performance	Total (14 criteria)	Relative Decimal Value
Best use of hardware	■	.20	.10	.20	3.7	.01
Ease of use	5.0	■	.20	.20	35.4	.08
Maximum functionality	10.0	5.0	■	5.0	69.0	.17
Best performance	5.0	5.0	.20	■	45.2	.11
				Grand Total (14 criteria)	418.1	

Information provided courtesy of Novacor Chemicals

Note: This constructed example, illustrated on three pages, represents only a portion of the prioritization process and only a portion of Novacor's spreadsheet evaluation process. Novacor Chemicals assembled a 16-person team, comprised mainly of system users and some information systems staff. The team developed and weighted 14 standard criteria and then applied them to choices in word processing, spreadsheet, and presentation graphics programs.

This example continued on the next page

Prioritization

Choosing a Standard Corporate Spreadsheet Program (cont.)

② Comparing options (described in Step 4)
These are just 2 of 14 matrices.

Best integration –internal	Program A	Program B	Program C	Total	Relative Decimal Value
Program A		1.00	1.00	2.00	.33
Program B	1.00		1.00	2.00	.33
Program C	1.00	1.00		2.00	.33
			Grand Total	6.00	

Lowest ongoing cost	Program A	Program B	Program C	Total	Relative Decimal Value
Program A		.10	.20	.30	.02
Program B	10.00		5.00	15.00	.73
Program C	5.00	.20		5.20	.25
			Grand Total	20.50	

Information provided courtesy of Novacor Chemicals

This example continued on the next page

Prioritization
Choosing a Standard Corporate Spreadsheet Program (cont.)

③ Summarize Option Ratings Across All Criteria
(described in Step 5)

This is a portion of a full matrix with 14 criteria in total.

Criteria / Options	Easy to use (.08)	Best integration int. (.09)	Lowest ongoing cost (.08)	Total (across 14 criteria)	Relative Decimal Value
Program A	.03 (.01)	.33 (.03)	.02 (0)	.16	.18
Program B	.48 (.04)	.33 (.03)	.73 (.06)	.30	.33
Program C	.48 (.04)	.33 (.03)	.25 (.02)	.44	.49
			Grand Total	.90	

Information provided courtesy of Novacor Chemicals

Result: Program C was chosen. Even though 14 out of the 16 team members were not currently using this program, the prioritization process changed their minds, and prevented them from biasing the final decision.

198 Prioritization Matrices ©2002 GOAL/QPC

Process Management Chart

Ensuring your changes stay in place

Why use it?

To combine your plan for completing a work process together with the Check and Act phases of the PDCA Cycle and to monitor the implementation of the solutions you selected. (For details on the PDCA Cycle, see pages 11 through 13 of *The Problem Solving Memory Jogger™*.)

What does it do?

- Communicates the new process or procedures to other team members
- Indicates what type of corrective action will be taken when a trigger or indicator occurs

A Sample Process Management Chart

Plan/Do	Check	Act
Flowchart	Indicators	Corrective Actions
	Plot time on each order; should be ≤ two hours; check for special causes.	If time exceeds two hours, alert Sam immediately; organize investigation.
	Count errors.	If more than one per order, stop process and contact Sam.

The plan is typically captured as a flowchart. →

The middle column describes what you will check in the process to monitor its quality. →

The third column describes how the process operators should react, depending on what they find in the measures. →

Plan/Do	Check	Act
Flowchart	Indicators	Corrective Actions
[flowchart]	Plot time on each order; should be ≤ two hours; check for special causes.	If time exceeds two hours, alert Sam immediately; organize investigation.
	Count errors.	If more than one per order, stop process and contact Sam.

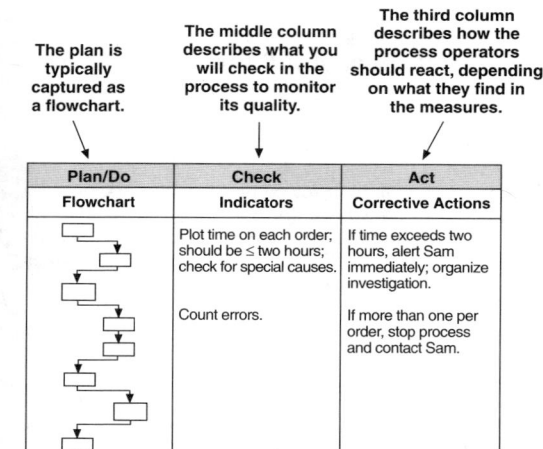

How do I do it?

1. Complete the Plan/Do section of the chart

- You can use any type of flowchart you want for the Plan/Do column. Typically, a Deployment Flowchart works best for administrative or service processes, while an Activity Flowchart works best for manufacturing processes.

- The key is to capture the essential steps of the process you are studying.

- For each key step, show how the operation should be done or provide a reference to a document that describes the step.

2. **Complete the Check section of the chart**
    - For manufacturing processes, the Check column often describes any technical specifications that have to be met. For administrative and service processes, this column usually describes quality criteria that have been defined for the process.
    - *Key process indicators* are the characteristics to be monitored in each critical step (e.g., elapsed time, completeness, presence of errors, temperature).
    - For each key process indicator, describe any important targets, numerical limits, tolerances, or specifications to which the process should conform if it is running well (e.g., eight hours from receipt, all boxes checked, 125°F–135°F). These standards can come from customers, regulatory policies, or process knowledge.
    - For each key process indicator, describe how the monitored data should be recorded (e.g., checklist, Run Chart, Control Chart, Scatter Diagram). Describe, if necessary, who should record the data and how.

3. **Complete the Act section of the chart**
    - Address damage control.
      - Who should do what with the output of the defective process?
      - What should be done for customers who receive the defective output?
      - What adjustments should be made to ensure that there will be no defects in the next iteration?

- Address procedures for process adjustment.
  - What must be done to gain sufficient understanding of this process so that the operators know what adjustments and accommodations are routinely necessary to prevent a recurrence of this problem?
- Address procedures for systems improvement.
  - Who in the organization needs what data in what form to be able to make a sound decision regarding new systems or remedies at deeper levels in the organization (i.e., changes in basic designs or policies)?

Tip In manufacturing, Process Management Charts typically include references to manufacturing specifications, physical attributes to be checked, and so on. By contrast, as shown in this example, administrative or service Process Management Charts are more often concerned with whose responsibility it is to carry out different tasks and what standards should be used for those tasks.

Example

An organization was having trouble with the processing of time-and-expense reports. A cross-functional group got together and agreed on who would do what, defined various codes and methods to be used, and created standard forms to be used. The cross-functional group used the document shown on the next page to communicate with all the organization's employees about the new procedures.

A Process Management Chart for Processing Expense Records

The Plan for Doing the Work — Flowchart	Checking the Work — Key Process Indicators	Act: Response to Results — Corrective Actions
Employee: Incurs expense and does activity. Completes white expense form and yellow timesheet. **Administrative Support**: Receives form; checks coding of expenses. Copy to HR; copy saved for invoicing; original & receipts to financial services. **Human Resources**: Records data. Prepares monthly report. **Financial Services**: Enters data into spreadsheet. Correct? — No: Resolve discrepancies. Yes: Issue check. **Management**	100% inspection for standards: 1. Received by 5 p.m. Tues. (on-site) or 5 p.m. Wed. (by mail). 2. Operational definitions of expenses used. 3. Complete information provided. 4. Columns added and summary completed. Receipts behind form, stapled in upper left corner. HR does 100% inspection for proper use of time-coding vacation, leave, and holiday expenses used. FS responsible for: 1. All charges allocated. 2. Proper use of budget codes.	Correct form or return to employee. Discuss corrections with employee. Provide training if needed. Correct form or return to employee. Discuss corrections with employee. Provide training if needed. If unclear about budget codes, check with manager. If incorrect: 1. Work with Administrative Support to resolve. 2. Track common areas of problems and report to manager monthly.

©2002 GOAL/QPC   **Process Management Chart**   203

Process Sigma
Measuring performance from the customer's perspective

Why use it?

To measure how much variation there is in a process relative to customer specifications. The process-sigma value is based on the number of defects per million opportunities, or DPMO. It is an expression of process yield (based on the DPMO). If you find a lot of variation relative to customer specifications, your process has a low process-sigma value. If you find little variation relative to customer specifications, your process has a high process-sigma value.

Historical data indicates a change of 1.5 in a process-sigma value when short-and long-term process capabilities are compared. This shift is due to drift in the mean of a process over time, which increases overall process variation, thus reducing the sigma value. Typically, the short-term capability and sigma value are determined. Subtracting 1.5 from the short-term value provides a good estimate of long-term process capability based on short-term measurements. The tables in this section give the long-term sigma value for short-term data. To obtain the actual sigma value for the data, subtract 1.5 from the values shown.

What does it do?

- Provides a more sensitive indicator than percent yield. "Yield" refers to how much of your process output is acceptable to your customers. A 99% yield sounds good, but the 6,210 DPMO value at this quality level shows that there is significant room for improvement.

Process Sigma Values

These are estimates of long-term sigma values. For actual sigma values, subtract 1.5 from these values.

Percent	DPMO	σ
99%	6,210	4.0
99.87%	1,350	4.5
99.977%	233	5.0
99.9997%	3.4	6.0

- Focuses on defects. Even a single defect reflects a failure in your customers' eyes.
- Makes comparisons easier by using a common metric. Because the three processes in the table below are measured with different metrics, it is difficult to tell which process performed best.

Three Processes with Different Metrics

Process	Transactions per Month	Performance
Calls handled	14,000	Average 10% require transfers
Credits processed	75	Average cycle time of three days
Daily reports	28–31	Nine errors per day

How do I do it?

There are two methods for calculating process sigma. Method 1 involves looking up the actual yield in a process-sigma conversion table like the one at the end of this section. Method 2 involves looking up a normal approximation of yield in a process-sigma table. Method 1 is detailed below. If you need to use Method 2, see your Six Sigma Expert or Master Six Sigma Expert for pointers.

Method 1 for Calculating Process Sigma

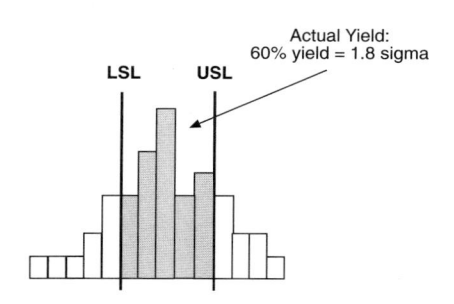

Actual Yield:
60% yield = 1.8 sigma

LSL USL

Method 2 for Calculating Process Sigma

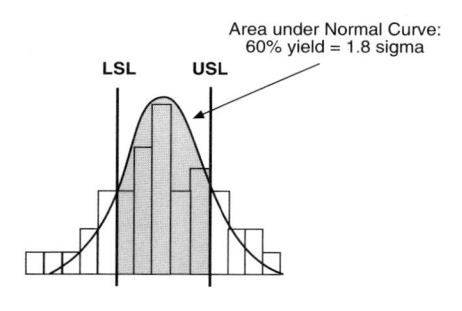

Area under Normal Curve:
60% yield = 1.8 sigma

LSL USL

Method 1

1. Review each of the Critical To Quality characteristics (CTQs) that you have selected for the project.

2. **For each CTQ, clearly define what a defect is.** In general, a defect is any aspect of a product or service that does not meet a customer specification. In some industries, a customer specification is also referred to as a *customer tolerance*.

3. **Define a defect opportunity ("O") for each CTQ.** In general, a defect opportunity is a measurable chance for a defect to occur.

   • A defect opportunity occurs each time the product, service, or information is handled. It is the point at which a customer quality requirement is either met or missed.

   Tip Remember that a defect opportunity is based on the quality characteristic that is not met—not on the number of ways in which it can be missed. For example, you should not list both "incorrect name" and "misspelled name" as defect opportunities for a form. Rather, list one defect opportunity associated with the quality characteristics of "correct name."

   Tip Whenever possible, stick with the same definitions of defect opportunities that were used in the past. The focus of process sigma is on improvement, and it is impossible to measure improvement if what you consider to be a defect is constantly changing.

   Tip Simple processes have few defect opportunities; complex processes have more. For example, a simple sub-process like posting a payment has only two defect opportunities: incorrect post and late post. More complex processes, like structuring a deal, have many more opportunities—perhaps one each for the accuracy and timeliness of key research figures, several for the timeliness and professionalism of key customer interactions, and so on. However, if the process sigma for complex processes in your organization has always been determined from a few simple defect opportunities determined by the customer, it might be best not to change your measurement system.

Tip Make sure that you count only those defects that can be reasonably expected to happen or that have happened in the past. Also make sure that each defect opportunity matters to the customer.

Tip It is important for the number of defect opportunities to remain constant throughout your analysis. The number of opportunities is an ingredient of the yield calculation used to determine process sigma. If the number of opportunities changes, your calculations of yield before and after a change won't be comparable.

Sample Yield-Calculation Factors

Situation	CTQ	Unit	Defect Opportunities per Unit
Credit card bill	Accurate amounts	Each bill	One per transaction
	Correct address	Each bill	One per bill

4. Determine the number of units produced ("N"). A unit is the item produced or processed.

5. Determine the total number of defects made ("D"). Include any defects that are made and then later fixed. By including the defects that later get fixed, you are calculating your process sigma based on the first-pass yield of the process, not the final yield. The first-pass yield provides the most accurate picture of the process because:

   - It is difficult to "inspect away" defects.
   - It is very costly to fix errors.
   - It reveals a process's true improvement potential.

First-Pass Yield vs. Final Yield

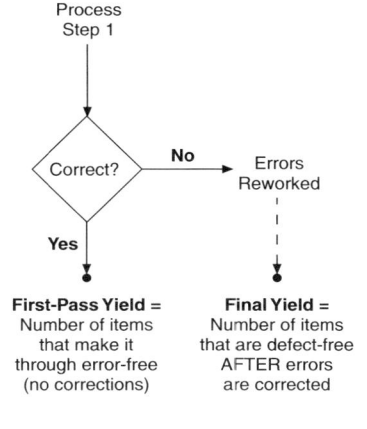

```
          Process
          Step 1
             │
             ▼
         ┌───────┐    No
         │Correct?│─────────▶  Errors
         └───────┘            Reworked
           │ Yes                 │
           ▼                     ▼
   First-Pass Yield =       Final Yield =
   Number of items         Number of items
   that make it            that are defect-free
   through error-free      AFTER errors
   (no corrections)        are corrected
```

6. Calculate defects per opportunity ("DPO"). DPO = D/(N × O).
7. Calculate yield. Yield = (1 − DPO) × 100.
8. Look up your process sigma in the Process-Sigma Conversion Table on page 212.

Example:

A Sample Process-Sigma Calculation

```
100 units
  2 opportunities
    per unit
  7 defects
```

$$\text{Yield} = \left(1 - \frac{7}{100 \times 2}\right) \times 100$$

$$= (1 - .035) \times 100 = 96.5\% = 3.3\,\sigma \text{ (long-term)}$$

1. Determine number of defect opportunities per unit.	O =	2
2. Determine number of units processed.	N =	100
3. Determine total number of defects made; include defects made and later fixed.	D =	7
4. Calculate defects per opportunity.	$\text{DPO} = \dfrac{D}{N \times O} =$	.035
5. Calculate yield.	$\text{Yield} = (1 - \text{DPO}) \times 100 =$	96.5
6. Look up process sigma in the conversion table.	Long-term process sigma =	3.3
	Actual process sigma =	1.8

Tip Method 1 is reliable only if there is a sufficient number of defects and non-defects. You must have at least five of each category for this method to work.

Tip In some cases the main concern is with the overall process yield only. In such cases, set one specification for the process as a whole, and determine one overall process-sigma cycle time for the entire process (e.g., "complete the process within three days").

In other cases, there might be separate specifications for different steps. Then you need to know how to determine the process sigma for each step and combine them into an overall process sigma for the entire process.

Process-Sigma Conversion Table

These are estimates of long-term sigma values. For actual sigma values, subtract 1.5 from these values.

Yield	DPMO	Process Sigma	Yield	DPMO	Process Sigma
99.9999%	1	6.27	92.00%	80,000	2.91
99.9997%	3	6.04	91.00%	90,000	2.84
99.9990%	10	5.77	90.00%	100,000	2.78
99.99%	100	5.22	85.00%	150,000	2.54
99.90%	1,000	4.59	80.00%	200,000	2.34
99.80%	2,000	4.38	75.00%	250,000	2.17
99.70%	3,000	4.25	70.00%	300,000	2.02
99.60%	4,000	4.15	65.00%	350,000	1.89
99.50%	5,000	4.08	60.00%	400,000	1.75
99.40%	6,000	4.01	55.00%	450,000	1.63
99.30%	7,000	3.96	50.00%	500,000	1.50
99.20%	8,000	3.91	45.00%	550,000	1.37
99.10%	9,000	3.87	40.00%	600,000	1.25
99.00%	10,000	3.83	35.00%	650,000	1.11
98.00%	20,000	3.55	30.00%	700,000	0.98
97.00%	30,000	3.38	25.00%	750,000	0.83
96.00%	40,000	3.25	20.00%	800,000	0.66
95.00%	50,000	3.14	15.00%	850,000	0.46
94.00%	60,000	3.05	10.00%	900,000	0.22
93.00%	70,000	2.98			

Yield Conversion Table

These are estimates of long-term sigma values. For actual sigma values, subtract 1.5 from these values.

Sigma	DPMO	Yield	Sigma	DPMO	Yield
6	3.4	99.99966%	2.9	80,757	91.9%
5.9	5.4	99.99946%	2.8	96,801	90.3%
5.8	8.5	99.99915%	2.7	115,070	88.5%
5.7	13	99.99866%	2.6	135,666	86.4%
5.6	21	99.9979%	2.5	158,655	84.1%
5.5	32	99.9968%	2.4	184,060	81.6%
5.4	48	99.9952%	2.3	211,855	78.8%
5.3	72	99.9928%	2.2	241,964	75.8%
5.2	108	99.9892%	2.1	274,253	72.6%
5.1	159	99.984%	2	308,538	69.1%
5	233	99.977%	1.9	344,578	65.5%
4.9	337	99.966%	1.8	382,089	61.8%
4.8	483	99.952%	1.7	420,740	57.9%
4.7	687	99.931%	1.6	460,172	54.0%
4.6	968	99.90%	1.5	500,000	50.0%
4.5	1,350	99.87%	1.4	539,828	46.0%
4.4	1,866	99.81%	1.3	579,260	42.1%
4.3	2,555	99.74%	1.2	617,911	38.2%
4.2	3,467	99.65%	1.1	655,422	34.5%
4.1	4,661	99.53%	1	691,462	30.9%
4	6,210	99.38%	0.9	725,747	27.4%
3.9	8,198	99.18%	0.8	758,036	24.2%
3.8	10,724	98.9%	0.7	788,145	21.2%
3.7	13,903	98.6%	0.6	815,940	18.4%
3.6	17,864	98.2%	0.5	841,345	15.9%
3.5	22,750	97.7%	0.4	864,334	13.6%
3.4	28,716	97.1%	0.3	884,930	11.5%
3.3	35,930	96.4%	0.2	903,199	9.7%
3.2	44,565	95.5%	0.1	919,243	8.1%
3.1	54,799	94.5%			
3	66,807	93.3%			

Regression
Quantifying the relationship between two variables

Why use it?
To investigate suspected correlations by generating an equation that quantifies the relationship.

What does it do?
- Explains the relationship through an equation for a line, curve, or surface
- Explains the variation in y values
- Enables you to predict the impact of controlling a process variable (x)
- Enables you to predict future process performance for certain values of x
- Helps you identify the vital few x's that drive y (see the section on the y = f (x) formula)
- Helps you manipulate process conditions to generate desirable results (if x is controllable) and/or avoid undesirable results

For linear regressions (i.e., when the relationship is defined by a line), the regression equation is represented as $y = b_0 + b_1x$, where b_0 = intercept (i.e., the point where the line crosses x = 0) and b_1 = slope (i.e., rise over run, or change in y per unit increase in x).

Note: You might be accustomed to expressing the equation for a line as y = mx + b, where m = slope and b = intercept. We use a different notation here, for reasons that will become clear when you do multiple regression. (See the graph at the end of this section.)

An Example of Linear Regression

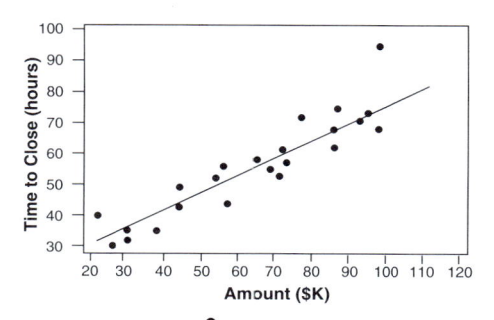

How do I do it?

Use the least squares method, where you determine the regression equation by using a procedure that minimizes the total squared distance from all points to the line.

This method finds the line where the squared vertical distance from each data point to the line is as small as possible (or the "least"). This means that the method minimizes the "square" of all the residuals.

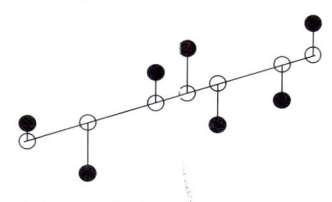

Least squares method
1. Measure vertical distance from points to line.
2. Square the figures.
3. Sum the total squared distance.
4. Find the line that minimizes that sum.

Data (both x and y values) are used to obtain the b_0 and b_1 values, and the b_0 and b_1 values establish the equation.

1. **Plot the data on a Scatter Diagram (see page 228 for details)**

    Tip Be sure to plot your data before doing regression. The charts below show four sets of data that have the same regression equation: $y = 3 + 0.5x$. Obviously, there are four completely different relationships.

Four Plots of the Same Equation

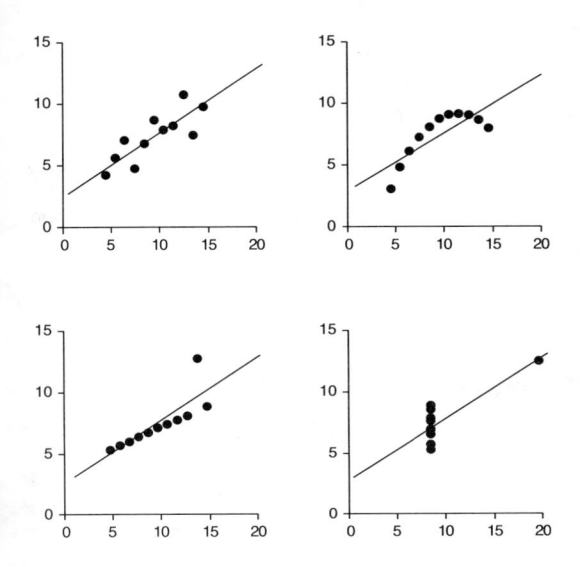

216 Regression

2. **Measure the vertical distance from the points to the line**
3. **Square the figures**
4. **Sum the total squared distance**
5. **Find the line that minimizes the sum**

> **Tip** Generally a computer program is used to generate the "best fit" line that represents the relationship between x and y. This work is typically performed by a Six Sigma Expert and is shown here for overview purposes only.

> **Tip** The following sets of terms are often used interchangeably:
> - Regression equation and regression line.
> - Prediction equation and prediction line.
> - Fitted line, or fits, and model.

> **Tip** When two variables show a relationship on a scatter plot, they are said to be correlated, but this does not necessarily mean they have a cause/effect relationship. *Correlation* means two things vary together. *Causation* means changes in one variable cause changes in the other.

Correlated Variables

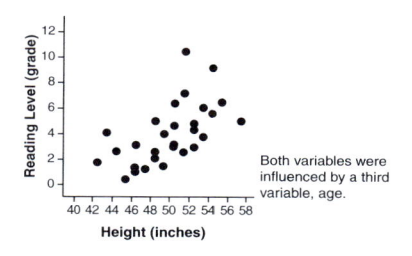

Both variables were influenced by a third variable, age.

> **Tip** *Extrapolation* refers to making predictions outside the range of the x data. It's a natural desire, but it can be very risky. Predictions from regression equations are more reliable for x's within the range of the observed data. Extrapolation is less risky if you have a theory, process knowledge, or other data to guide you.

An Example of Extrapolation

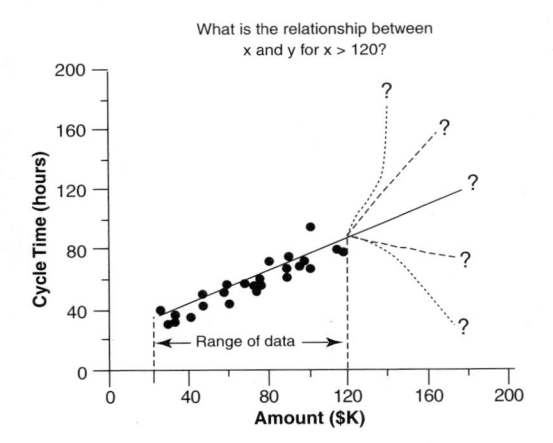

What is the relationship between x and y for x > 120?

[Scatter plot showing Cycle Time (hours) vs. Amount ($K), with data ranging from about 20 to 120 on the x-axis, and multiple dashed lines with "?" marks extending beyond x = 120 in various directions.]

The residual is the leftover variation in y after you use x to predict y. The residual represents common-cause (i.e., random and unexplained) variation. You determine a residual by subtracting the predicted y from the observed y.

Residuals are assumed to have the following properties:
- Not related to the x's.
- Stable, independent, and not changing over time.
- Constant and not increasing as the predicted y's increase.
- Normal (i.e., bell-shaped) with a mean of zero.

An Example of Residuals

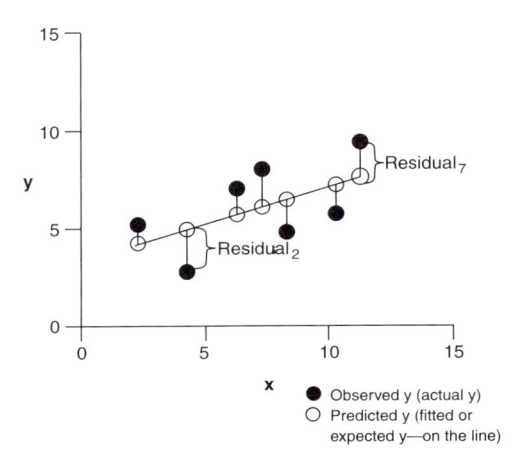

[Scatter plot showing observed y values (filled circles) and predicted y values (open circles) on a fitted line, with Residual₂ and Residual₇ labeled as the vertical distances between observed and predicted values. X-axis ranges from 0 to 15, y-axis ranges from 0 to 15.]

● Observed y (actual y)
○ Predicted y (fitted or expected y—on the line)

Your Six Sigma Expert will be responsible for checking each of these assumptions. If the assumptions do not hold, the regression equation might be incorrect or misleading.

Tip Other types of regression your team might need to use are shown in the following graph.

Other Types of Regression

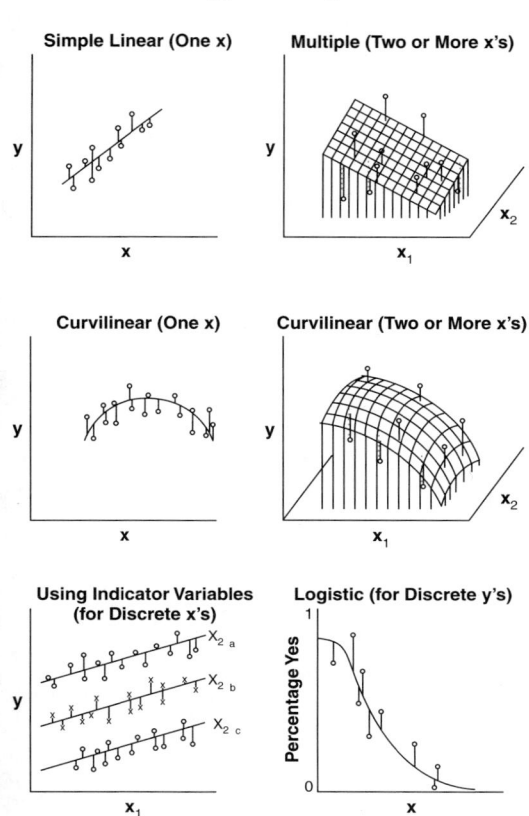

Simple Linear (One x)

Multiple (Two or More x's)

Curvilinear (One x)

Curvilinear (Two or More x's)

Using Indicator Variables (for Discrete x's)

Logistic (for Discrete y's)

220 Regression

Run Chart
Tracking trends

Why use it?
To allow a team to study observed data from a Check Sheet or other data-collection source to analyze trends or patterns over a specified period of time.

What does it do?
- Monitors the performance of one or more processes over time to detect trends, shifts, or cycles
- Allows a team to compare a performance measure before and after implementation of a solution to measure its impact
- Focuses attention on vital changes in the process
- Tracks useful information for predicting trends

How do I do it?

1. **Decide on the process performance measure**

2. **Gather data**
   - Generally, collect 20–25 data points to detect meaningful patterns.

3. **Create a graph with a vertical line (y axis) and a horizontal line (x axis)**
   - On the vertical line (y axis), draw the scale related to the variable you are measuring.
     - Arrange the y axis to cover the full range of the measurements and then some, e.g., $1\frac{1}{2}$ times the range of data.
   - On the horizontal line (x axis), draw the time or sequence scale.

4. Plot the data

- Look at the data collected. If there are no obvious trends, calculate the average or arithmetic mean. The average is the sum of the measured values divided by the number of data points. The median value can also be used but the mean is the most frequently used measure of the "centering" of the sample. (See Data Points for more information on averages.) Draw a horizontal line at the average value.

Tip Do not redraw this line every time new data is added. Only when there has been a major change in the process or prevailing conditions should the average be recalculated and redrawn, and then only using the data points after the verified change.

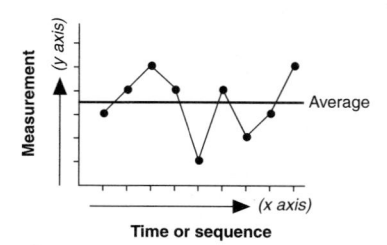

5. Interpret the Chart

- Note the position of the average line. Is it where it should be relative to a customer need or specification? Is it where you want it relative to your business objective?

Tip A danger in using a Run Chart is the tendency to see every variation in data as being important. The Run Chart should be used to focus on truly vital changes in the process. Simple tests can be used to look for meaningful trends and patterns. These tests are found in the Control Charts section. Remember that for more sophisticated uses, a Control Chart is invaluable since it is simply a Run Chart with statistically based limits.

Variation

Like Control Charts, Run Charts can be used to assess whether there are any signs of special-cause variation. In general, to use a Run Chart you follow five steps:

1. **Collect twenty or more data values over time.**
2. **Plot the data in time order.**
3. **Pencil in the median line.**
4. **Count the runs above and below the median. A *run* is a series of points on the same side of the median; a series can be of any length, from one point to many points.**
5. **Check for special causes.**

If you see any signs of a special cause, try to determine what it is and then work to remove it permanently. If the process is stable, continue with your data analysis.

Sample Run Chart

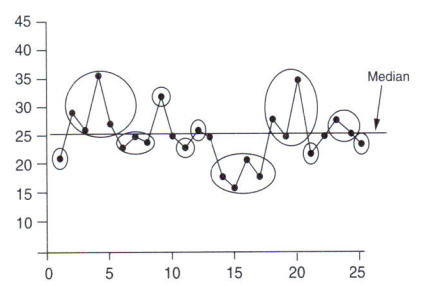

Twenty data points not on median out of eleven runs

Note: Points on the median are ignored. They do not add to or interrupt a run.

A run ends anytime the connecting line crosses the median. The number of runs you should expect to see in a stable process depends on the number of data points. The chart below shows how many runs you can expect when only common-cause variation is present. The twenty data points not on the median for eleven runs in the sample Run Chart is well within the range listed in the chart below. Thus, based on this test, you can reasonably conclude there are no special causes of variation.

Expected Numbers of Runs

Number of Data Points Not on Median	Lower Limit for Number of Runs	Upper Limit for Number of Runs	Number of Data Points Not on Median	Lower Limit for Number of Runs	Upper Limit for Number of Runs
10	3	8	34	12	23
11	3	9	35	13	23
12	3	10	36	13	24
13	4	10	37	13	25
14	4	11	38	14	25
15	4	12	39	14	26
16	5	12	40	15	26
17	5	13	41	16	26
18	6	13	42	16	27
19	6	14	43	17	27
20	6	14	44	17	28
21	7	15	45	17	29
22	7	16	46	17	30
23	8	16	47	18	30
24	8	17	48	18	31
25	9	17	49	19	31
26	9	18	50	19	32
27	9	19	60	24	37
28	10	19	70	28	43
29	10	20	80	33	48
30	11	20	90	37	54
31	11	21	100	42	59
32	11	22	110	46	65
33	11	22	120	51	70

In addition to checking the number of runs, other tests for special causes you can use with Run Charts are as follows:

- Too many runs.
- Too few runs.
- Six or more points in a row continuously increasing or decreasing. This indicates a trend.
- Eight or more points in a row on the same side of the median. This indicates a shift. When counting runs on the same side of the center line, ignore any points on the center line.
- Fourteen or more points in a row alternating up and down. When counting runs up or down, ignore any points that repeat the preceding value. If two points in a row have the same value, ignore the second point.

Below are illustrations of each of these special causes:

Other Tests for Special Causes

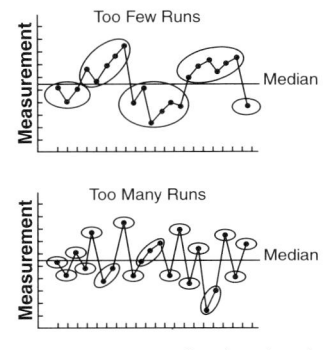

Continued on the next page

Other Tests for Special Causes (cont.)

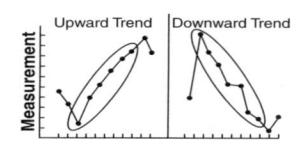

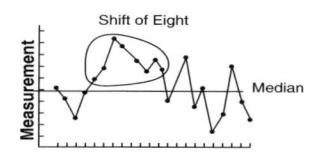

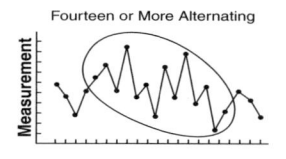

Run

Average Number of Days for Determining Eligibility for Services

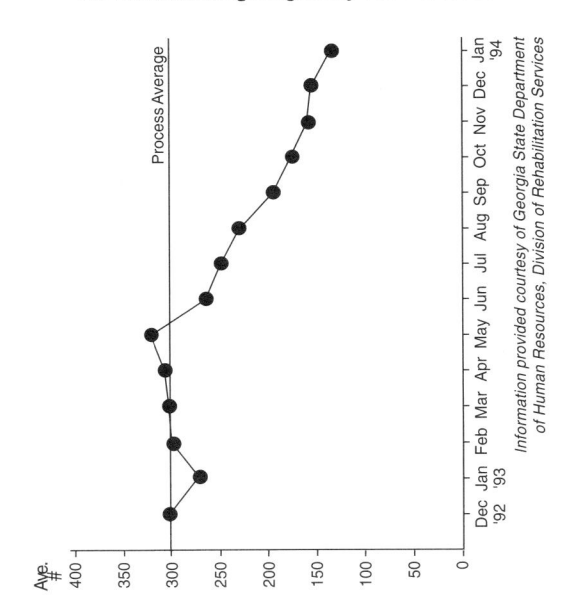

Information provided courtesy of Georgia State Department of Human Resources, Division of Rehabilitation Services

Note: Eligibility requirements changed in May, making it much simpler for the department staff to make determinations. The trend is statistically significant because there are six or more consecutive points declining.

©2002 GOAL/QPC   Run Chart **227**

Scatter Diagram
Measuring relationships between variables

Why use it?

To study and identify the possible relationship between the changes observed in two different sets of variables.

What does it do?

- Supplies the data to confirm a hypothesis that two variables are related
- Provides both a visual and statistical means to test the strength of a potential relationship
- Provides a good follow-up to a Cause & Effect Diagram to find out if there is more than just a consensus connection between causes and the effect

How do I do it?

1. **Collect 50–100 paired samples of data that you think may be related and construct a data sheet**

Course	Average Session Rating (on a 1–5 scale)	Average Experience of Training Team (days)
1	4.2	220
2	3.7	270
3	4.3	270
•	•	•
•	•	•
•	•	•
40	3.9	625

Theory: There is a possible relationship between the number of days of experience the training team has received and the ratings of course sessions.

2. Draw the horizontal (x axis) and vertical (y axis) lines of the diagram

- The measurement scales generally increase as you move up the vertical axis and to the right on the horizontal axis.

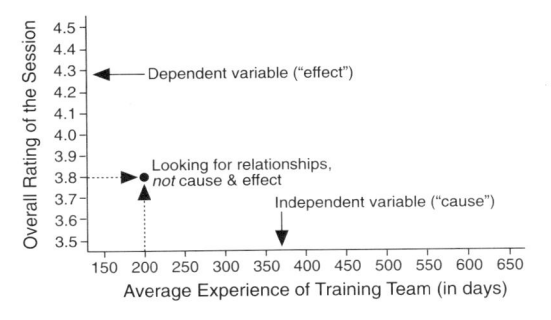

Overall Rating of the Session (y-axis: 3.5 to 4.5)
- 4.3 ← Dependent variable ("effect")
- 3.8 ← Looking for relationships, *not* cause & effect
- Independent variable ("cause")

Average Experience of Training Team (in days) (x-axis: 150 to 650)

3. Plot the data on the diagram

- If values are repeated, circle that point as many times as is appropriate.

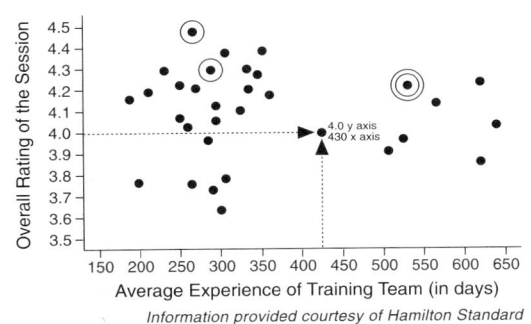

4.0 y axis
430 x axis

Average Experience of Training Team (in days)

Information provided courtesy of Hamilton Standard

©2002 GOAL/QPC

Scatter Diagram 229

4. **Interpret the data**
   - There are many levels of analysis that can be applied to Scatter Diagram data. Any basic statistical process control text, like Kaoru Ishikawa's *Guide to Quality Control*, describes additional correlation tests. It is important to note that all of the examples in this chapter are based on straight-line correlations. There are a number of non-linear patterns that can be routinely encountered, e.g., $y = e^x$, $y = x^2$. These types of analyses are beyond the scope of this book.
   - The following five illustrations show the various patterns and meanings that Scatter Diagrams can have. The example used is the training session assessment previously shown. The patterns have been altered for illustrative purposes. Pattern #3 is the actual sample.

   Tip The Scatter Diagram *does not predict* cause-and-effect relationships. It only shows the strength of the relationship between two variables. The stronger the relationship, the greater the likelihood that change in one variable will affect change in another variable.

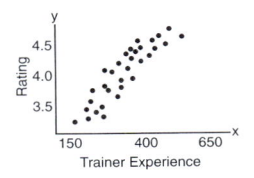

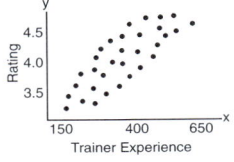

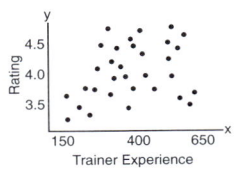

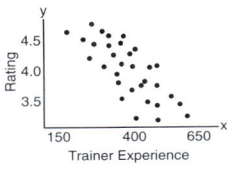

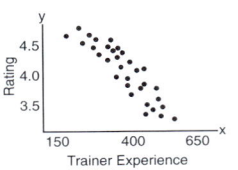

1. Positive Correlation. An increase in y may depend on an increase in x. Session ratings are likely to increase as trainer experience increases.

2. Possible Positive Correlation. If x is increased, y may increase somewhat. Other variables may be involved in the level of rating in addition to trainer experience.

3. No Correlation. There is no demonstrated connection between trainer experience and session ratings.

4. Possible Negative Correlation. As x is increased, y may decrease somewhat. Other variables, besides trainer experience, may also be affecting ratings.

5. Negative Correlation. A decrease in y may depend on an increase in x. Session ratings are likely to fall as trainer experience increases.

Variations

Stratifying a Scatter Diagram

You can stratify Scatter Diagrams to uncover clues about relationships between variables. In the example below, when the data is stratified by branch, no relationship is apparent between mistakes made on invoices and cycle time. Without stratification, mistakes made on invoices would have been mistakenly believed to be related to cycle time, when the actual relationship is between branch and cycle time.

A Stratified Scatter Diagram

After stratifying the plot, we see no correlation, but a difference due to branch.

Scatter Diagram Matrix

Many statistical software packages enable you to produce a matrix showing multiple Scatter Diagrams on one graph, called a Scatter Diagram Matrix. To continue the example mentioned above, the team finds that the average hold times are related to daily call volume. The team then decides to investigate whether hold times are also related to production hours (i.e., the number of hours staffed).

The following Scatter Diagram Matrix helps the team determine if there is a relationship among hold time, production hours, and call volume.

A Scatter Diagram Matrix

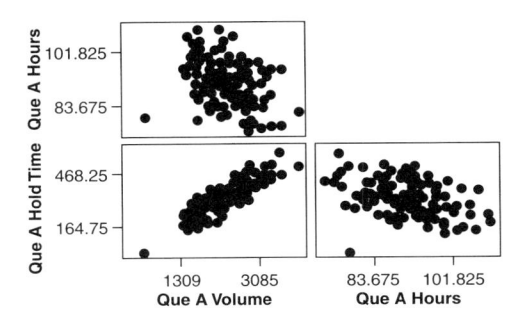

In the lower left diagram, the data points hug a diagonal line going from low values for each variable to high values, indicating a strong positive relationship between call volume and hold time. The other two diagrams show weaker negative relationships between the other variables: Higher call-volume values seem to be associated with lower values of production hours, and higher values of production hours seem to be associated with lower hold-time values.

Scatter

Capacitance vs. Line Width

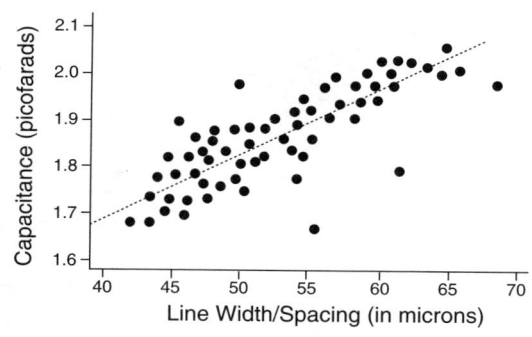

Information provided courtesy of AT&T

Note: This Scatter Diagram shows that there is a strong positive relationship between these two variables in producing microelectronic circuits. Since capacitance measures a critical performance of a circuit, anything that affects it positively or negatively is also critical. The diagram shows that line width/spacing is something to watch closely, perhaps using a Control Chart or another type of statistical process control (SPC) tool.

---

234 Scatter Diagram ©2002 GOAL/QPC

SIPOC
Understanding the process at a high level

Why use it?

To develop a high-level understanding of the process that is under study, including the upstream and downstream links.

What does it do?

- Defines project boundaries (i.e., starting and ending points)
- Describes where to collect data
- Identifies suppliers and customers (i.e., stakeholders who need to be considered as part of your project)
- Identifies inputs and outputs (i.e., what is flowing in and flowing out of the process)
- Helps to support process thinking within your organization

The SIPOC Process

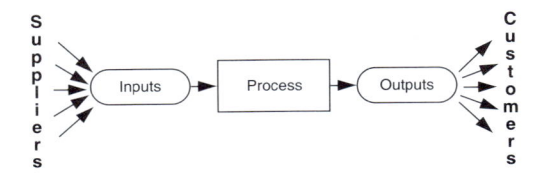

Suppliers → Inputs → Process → Outputs → Customers

How do I do it?

Many teams have trouble working on a SIPOC (Suppliers, Inputs, Process, Outputs, and Customers) diagram in order (i.e., starting with Suppliers and then moving onto Inputs, and so on). The following steps are often a more useful sequence for identifying SIPOC elements.

1. **Start by identifying the starting and ending points of the process you are studying**

2. **State the purpose of the process. Ask:**
   - Why does this process exist?
   - What is the purpose of this process?
   - What is the outcome?

3. **Fill in the main process steps between the starting and ending points so you have a total of five to seven steps. Think of your diagram as a top-level flowchart, where the focus is on main steps, not details. Here you are not concerned with loops or errors. To identify the main steps in the process, ask the following questions:**
   - What happens to each input?
   - What conversion activities take place?

   Tip When doing a SIPOC analysis, be sure to keep the process to between five and seven steps. You want to portray an overall picture of the major actions that occur in the process, not delve into details.

4. **Identify outputs from the process. Outputs can include physical products, documents, information, services, and decisions. To identify outputs, ask the following questions:**

- What product does this process make?
- At what point does this process end?
- What information does this process produce?

5. **Identify the customers for each output by asking:**
   - Who uses the products/information supplied from this process?
   - Who are the customers of this process?

6. **Identify the key process inputs. Here it helps to try to think of what actually flows through your process and what is being transformed. Is it a physical part or raw materials? A form? Documentation? A sample? Most process inputs are primarily in the form of materials and information, but they can also include ideas, labor, and environment. To identify inputs, ask:**
   - What flows into the process?
   - What triggers the process to start?

7. **Identify the key suppliers for each input by asking:**
   - Where does the information or material we work on come from? Who are our suppliers?
   - What do they supply?
   - Where do they affect the process flow?
   - What effect do they have on the process and on the outcome?

   Tip Some suppliers might provide more than one input, and a process often has more than one output.

A Sample SIPOC Diagram

Making a Photocopy

Suppliers	Inputs	Process	Outputs	Customers
		Put original on glass		You
Office supply company	Paper; copier setup	Close lid	Copies	File
Yourself	Original	Adjust settings		Others
		Press START		
		Remove originals and copies		

Tip After you complete the SIPOC diagram for your project, take a few minutes to review the charter and make any modifications that you think are appropriate.

Six Sigma Storyboard
Maintaining records and communicating progress

Why use it?
To track data, decisions, and actions and create a graphical or pictorial record of your DMAIC project.

What does it do?
- Facilitates decision making
- Helps maintain forward momentum
- Helps prevent rework
- Because they provide a quick, visual summary of a team's work, the elements of a Storyboard can also be used as presentation materials. Many organizations keep them permanently on record so other employees can have access to the improvement team's work.

How do I do it?

1. **Maintain records throughout the life of your project**
   - Agendas and meeting notes provide a permanent record of what issues are discussed at meetings—particularly what "to do" items are generated and what decisions are reached.
   - Records of customer interviews or surveys provide verbal data that will help to shape your effort. Your management sponsor or others in the organization might find this data helpful to also use for future efforts.

- Data-collection sheets provide the source for your analysis. You should keep them at least until the project is completed.
- Plans help you identify the components of a task, track your progress, and communicate your progress to others. Documented plans help you evaluate whether you did what you intended to do; they can also provide the basis for standardized work plans.
- Data charts help you understand your data, enable you to compare the outcome of the improvement effort with the initial situation, and provide a baseline for monitoring the process and making future improvements.

2. **Create a Six Sigma Storyboard**
    - Develop a pictorial record of the DMAIC steps by using the template on pages 241–243.

    Tip Keep your text brief, use a lot of graphics, and make sure your graphics effectively communicate your message.

3. **Present your Storyboard to others**

    Process-sigma project participants are often asked to introduce others in the organization to improvement concepts, explain a concept or tool they used, and present examples of their applications of various concepts and tools. Often this is done as a formal presentation.

Storyboard Template

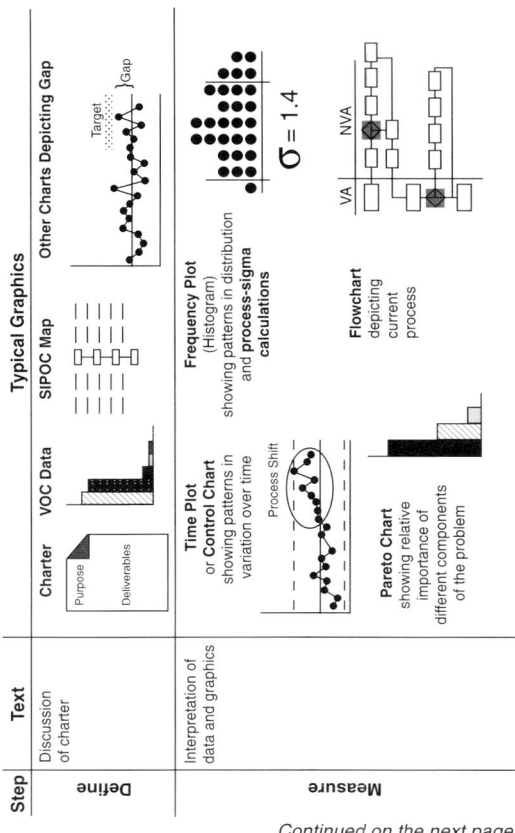

Step	Text	Typical Graphics			
Define	Discussion of charter	**Charter** (Purpose, Deliverables)	**VOC Data**	**SIPOC Map**	**Other Charts Depicting Gap** (Target, Gap)
Measure	Interpretation of data and graphics	**Time Plot** or **Control Chart** showing patterns in variation over time (Process Shift)	**Pareto Chart** showing relative importance of different components of the problem	**Frequency Plot** (Histogram) showing patterns in distribution and **process-sigma calculations** ($\sigma = 1.4$)	**Flowchart** depicting current process (VA / NVA)

Continued on the next page

©2002 GOAL/QPC   Six Sigma Storyboard 241

Storyboard Template (cont.)

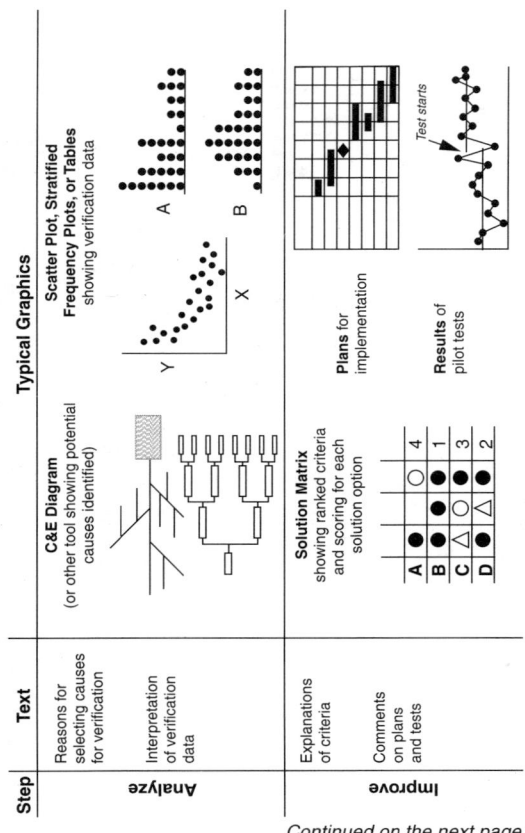

Step	Text	Typical Graphics
Analyze	Reasons for selecting causes for verification / Interpretation of verification data	**C&E Diagram** (or other tool showing potential causes identified) / **Scatter Plot, Stratified Frequency Plots, or Tables** showing verification data
Improve	Explanations of criteria / Comments on plans and tests	**Solution Matrix** showing ranked criteria and scoring for each solution option / **Plans** for implementation / **Results** of pilot tests

Continued on the next page

242 Six Sigma Storyboard ©2002 GOAL/QPC

Storyboard Template (cont.)

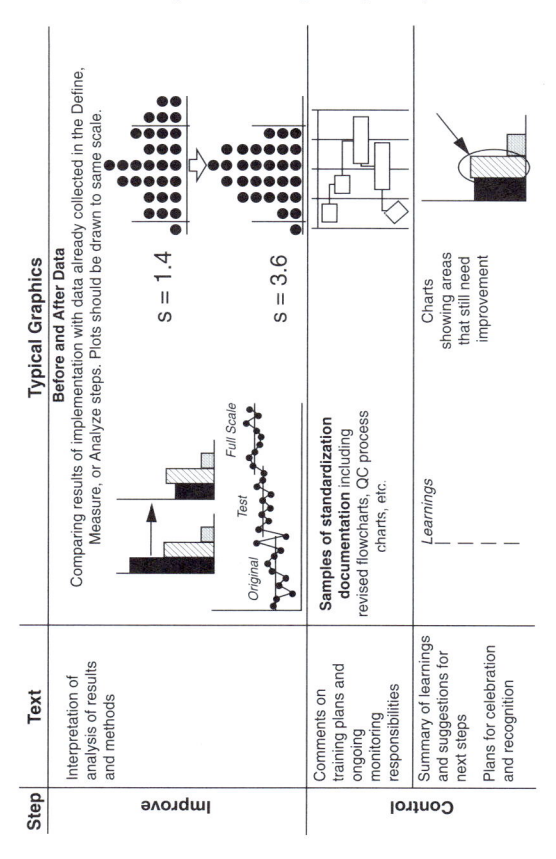

Step	Text	Typical Graphics
Improve	Interpretation of analysis of results and methods	**Before and After Data** Comparing results of implementation with data already collected in the Define, Measure, or Analyze steps. Plots should be drawn to same scale. $s = 1.4$ $s = 3.6$ *Original* — *Test* — *Full Scale*
Control	Comments on training plans and ongoing monitoring responsibilities	**Samples of standardization documentation** including revised flowcharts, QC process charts, etc.
Control	Summary of learnings and suggestions for next steps Plans for celebration and recognition	Charts showing areas that still need improvement *Learnings*

©2002 GOAL/QPC   Six Sigma Storyboard 243

Taguchi Loss Function
Reducing variation around a customer target

Why use it?

To understand the benefit of continually reducing variation, even when customer specifications are met.

What does it do?

- Conceptually defines the loss associated with variation
- Illustrates the difference between variation and specifications. The amount of *variation* in a process tells you what the process is capable of achieving. *Specifications* tell you what you want a process to be able to achieve.
- Describes why meeting customer specifications is not enough

Traditionally, organizations focused only on achieving product and service levels that were within the customer-specified range (often called specifications, tolerances, or requirements). Under that mind-set, anything that fell within the limits was thought to be equally good; as long as the product or service was within customer specifications, there was no loss.

However, Genichi Taguchi, a renowned Japanese scholar, taught the business world that there is loss any time a product or service varies from a defined target. This loss comes from sources that include the following:

- Increased wear or decreased performance from parts that don't fit together precisely.
- Increased service calls for repairs.

- Repeated calls for information or for re-delivery of a service.
- Loss resulting from excess waiting or from excess inventory when a product or service is not delivered at the specified time.

According to the traditional view (see the figure below), any value between the specifications is equally good. According to the Taguchi view, on the other hand, anytime a characteristic deviates from the target, some loss occurs. The bigger the deviation, the bigger the loss (Taguchi, 1960).

Loss: Traditional View vs. Taguchi View

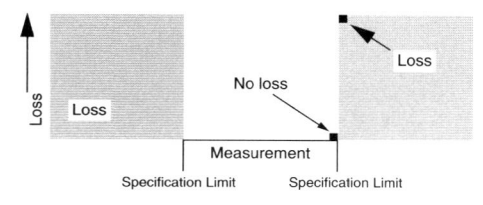

Taguchi Case Study

- In the 1980s, Ford Motor Company outsourced the construction of a subassembly to several of its own plants and to a Japanese manufacturer.
- Both the U.S. and Japan plants produced parts that conformed to specifications; both groups of parts had zero defects.
- Over the next few years, however, the number of warranty claims on the U.S.-built product was far higher than that for the Japanese product.
- The difference? The Japanese had worked to control and reduce variation—that is, get the parts as close to the actual target as possible. The U.S. plants had simply produced "within spec."
- The Japanese product was far more consistent; parts fit together better. The result: better performance and lower costs due to less scrap, less rework, and less inventory.

The Taguchi Case Study

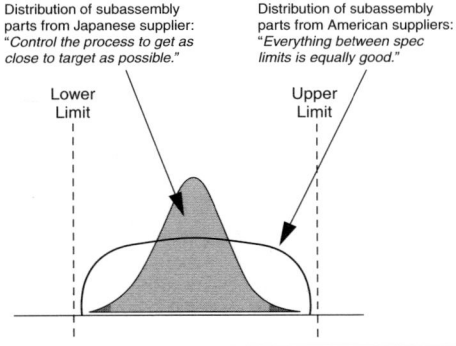

Distribution of subassembly parts from Japanese supplier: *"Control the process to get as close to target as possible."*

Distribution of subassembly parts from American suppliers: *"Everything between spec limits is equally good."*

Lower Limit

Upper Limit

Tollgate Review
Ensuring the project stays on track

Why use it?
To review progress and check for key deliverables at the completion of each step of the DMAIC method. The project sponsor reviews the Storyboard to make sure sufficient rigor has been used and provides a formal sign-off to show the step has been satisfactorily completed.

What does it do?
- Provides guidance and direction for the project team
- Establishes a common understanding of the efforts to date and enables you to monitor progress
- Ensures alignment and reinforces priorities
- Provides ongoing coaching and instruction about the project
- Recognizes the project team's efforts and fosters intrinsic motivation for improvements

How do I do it?

1. **A few days before the tollgate review, the project team prepares a Storyboard that shows the work completed for the current DMAIC step and sends it to the project sponsor. The sponsor then studies the Storyboard in preparation for the tollgate review.**

2. **During the tollgate review, the team members do the following:**
   - Present a brief background review to reiterate the project's purpose and importance.

- State the purpose of this tollgate review and highlight the required outcomes.
- Report on the project's progress since the last review. This includes doing the following:
  - Using the Storyboard as the presentation framework.
  - Emphasizing the logic of the work done during each step and conclusions drawn from analysis of the data.
  - Highlighting changes in the charter, expected results, or risks.
  - Presenting issues, options, decisions needed, or recommendations for discussion.
  - Presenting plans for next steps.

3. **After the presentation, the sponsor does the following:**
   - Reinforces the strengths of the team's work.
   - Asks questions about the team's logic and conclusions.
   - Offers reactions and suggestions, focusing on one or two specific suggestions for improving the logic or data.
   - Makes decisions.
   - Conveys appreciation for the team's progress.

4. **Before the review is over, the sponsor and the project team work together to:**
   - Review decisions, action items, and agreements about next steps.
   - Evaluate the review, identifying what was useful and any ways the review could be improved.

Tree Diagram
Mapping the tasks for implementation

Why use it?
To break any broad goal, graphically, into increasing levels of detailed actions that must or could be done to achieve the stated goals.

What does it do?
- Encourages team members to expand their thinking when creating solutions. Simultaneously, this tool keeps everyone linked to the overall goals and subgoals of a task
- Allows all participants (and reviewers outside the team) to check all of the logical links and completeness at every level of plan detail
- Moves the planning team from theory to the real world
- Reveals the *real* level of complexity involved in the achievement of any goal, making potentially overwhelming projects manageable, as well as uncovering unknown complexity

How do I do it?

1. **Choose the Tree Diagram goal statement**

   > Goal: Increase workplace suggestions

- Typical sources:
  - The root cause/driver identified in an Interrelationship Digraph (ID).
  - An Affinity Diagram with the headers as major subgoals.
  - Any assignment given to an individual or team.
- When used in conjunction with other management and planning tools, the most typical source is the root cause/driver identified in the ID.

Tip Regardless of the source, work hard to create—through consensus—a clear, action-oriented statement.

2. **Assemble the right team**
   - The team should consist of action planners with detailed knowledge of the goal topic. The team should take the Tree only to the level of detail that the team's knowledge will allow. Be prepared to hand further details to others.
   - Four to six people is the ideal group size, but the Tree Diagram is appropriate for larger groups as long as the ideas are visible and the session is well facilitated.

3. **Generate the major Tree headings, which are the major subgoals to pursue**
   - The simplest method for creating the highest, or first level of detail, is to brainstorm the major task areas. These are the major "means" by which the goal statement will be achieved.

- To encourage creativity, it is often helpful to do an "Action Affinity" on the goal statement. Brainstorm action statements and sort into groupings, but spend less time than usual refining the header cards. Use the header cards as the Tree's first-level subgoals.

Goal

Increase workplace suggestions

Means

Create a workable process

Create capability

Measure results

Provide recognition

Tip Use Post-it® Notes to create the levels of detail. Draw lines only when the Tree is finished. This allows it to stay flexible until the process is finished. The Tree can be oriented from left to right, right to left, or top down.

Tip Keep the first level of detail broad, and avoid jumping to the lowest level of task. Remember: "If you start with what you already know, you'll end up where you've already been."

4. Break each major heading into greater detail

- Working from the goal statement and first-level detail, placed either to the extreme left, right, or top of the work surface, ask of each first-level item, "What needs to be addressed to achieve the goal statement?"

  Repeat this question for each successive level of detail.

- Stop the breakdown of each level when there are assignable tasks or the team reaches the limit to its own expertise. Most Trees are broken out to the third level of detail (not counting the overall goal statement as a level). However, some subgoals are just simpler than others and don't require as much breakdown.

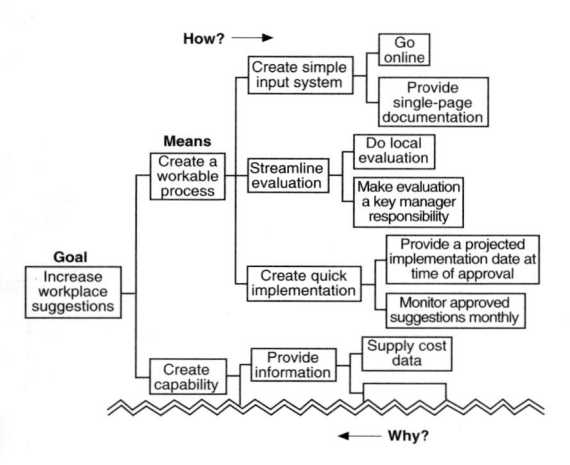

```
How? →

                                              ┌─ Go online
                        ┌─ Create simple ─────┤
                        │   input system      └─ Provide
                        │                        single-page documentation
              Means     │
           Create a ────┤                     ┌─ Do local evaluation
           workable     ├─ Streamline ────────┤
           process      │   evaluation        └─ Make evaluation
                        │                        a key manager responsibility
                        │
                        │                     ┌─ Provide a projected
   Goal                 └─ Create quick ──────┤   implementation date at
  Increase                  implementation    │   time of approval
  workplace                                   └─ Monitor approved
  suggestions                                     suggestions monthly

           Create ──── Provide ──── Supply cost
           capability  information  data

                                          ← Why?
```

252 Tree Diagram   ©2002 GOAL/QPC

5. **Review the completed Tree Diagram for logical flow and completeness**
    - At each level of detail, ask, "Is there something obvious that we have forgotten?"
    - As the Tree breaks down into greater detail (from general to specific) ask, "If I want to accomplish these results, do I really need to do these tasks?"
    - As the Tree builds into broader goals (from the specific to the general) ask, "Will these actions actually lead to these results?"
    - Draw the lines connecting the tasks.

    Tip The Tree Diagram is a great communication tool. It can be used to get input from those outside the team. The team's final task is to consider proposed changes, additions, or deletions and to modify the Tree as is appropriate.

Variations

The Process Decision Program Chart (PDPC) is a valuable tool for improving implementation through contingency planning. The PDPC, based on the Tree Diagram, involves a few simple steps.

1. **Assemble a team closest to the implementation**

2. **Determine proposed implementation steps**
    - List 4–10 broad steps and place them in sequence in the first Tree level.

3. **Branch likely problems off each step**
    - Ask, "What could go wrong?"

4. **Branch possible and reasonable responses off each likely problem**

5. Choose the most effective countermeasures and build them into a revised plan

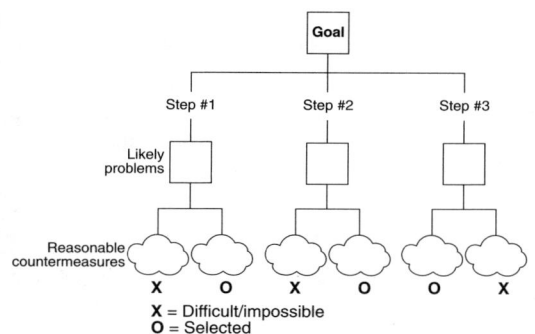

```
                        ┌──────┐
                        │ Goal │
                        └───┬──┘
              ┌─────────────┼─────────────┐
           Step #1        Step #2       Step #3
              │             │             │
           Likely
          problems □         □             □
              │             │             │
            ╭─╮╭─╮       ╭─╮╭─╮         ╭─╮╭─╮
Reasonable  ╰─╯╰─╯       ╰─╯╰─╯         ╰─╯╰─╯
countermeasures
             X   O         X   O         O   X
```

X = Difficult/impossible
O = Selected

PDPC (Tree Variation)

Awarding Unrestricted Financial Aid

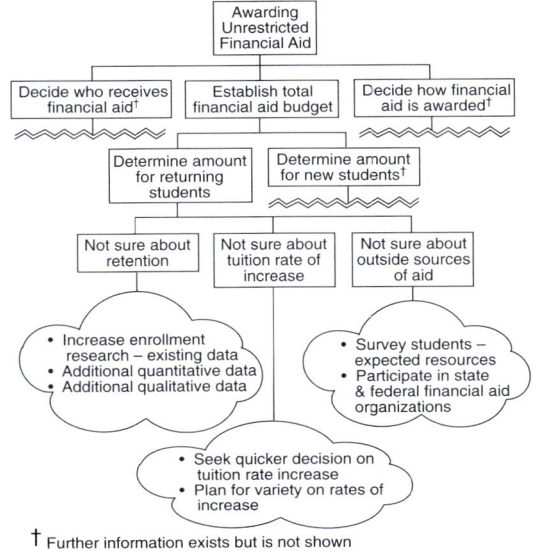

```
                    Awarding
                   Unrestricted
                  Financial Aid
                        |
    ┌───────────────────┼───────────────────┐
Decide who receives  Establish total   Decide how financial
 financial aid†      financial aid budget  aid is awarded†
~~~~~~~~~~~~~~~~         |           ~~~~~~~~~~~~~~~~
                ┌────────┴────────┐
          Determine amount   Determine amount
          for returning      for new students†
            students         ~~~~~~~~~~~~~~~~
                ┌────────────┬────────────┐
         Not sure about  Not sure about  Not sure about
           retention     tuition rate    outside sources
                         of increase     of aid
```

- Increase enrollment research – existing data
- Additional quantitative data
- Additional qualitative data

- Survey students – expected resources
- Participate in state & federal financial aid organizations

- Seek quicker decision on tuition rate increase
- Plan for variety on rates of increase

† Further information exists but is not shown

Information provided courtesy of St. John Fisher College

Note: The PDPC surfaced a lack of accurate information as a major problem. By anticipating this and filling the most critical information gaps, the budget can be more accurate.

Tree
Improve Business Planning Interaction

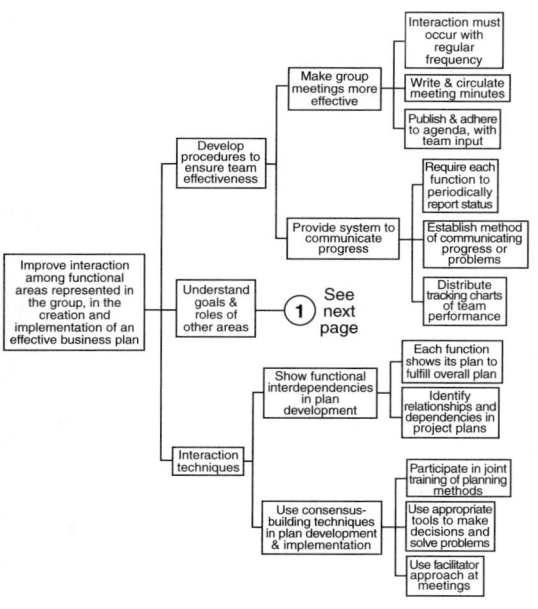

- **Improve interaction among functional areas represented in the group, in the creation and implementation of an effective business plan**
  - Develop procedures to ensure team effectiveness
    - Make group meetings more effective
      - Interaction must occur with regular frequency
      - Write & circulate meeting minutes
      - Publish & adhere to agenda, with team input
    - Provide system to communicate progress
      - Require each function to periodically report status
      - Establish method of communicating progress or problems
      - Distribute tracking charts of team performance
  - Understand goals & roles of other areas — (1) See next page
  - Interaction techniques
    - Show functional interdependencies in plan development
      - Each function shows its plan to fulfill overall plan
      - Identify relationships and dependencies in project plans
    - Use consensus-building techniques in plan development & implementation
      - Participate in joint training of planning methods
      - Use appropriate tools to make decisions and solve problems
      - Use facilitator approach at meetings

Information provided courtesy of Goodyear

Tree
Improve
Business Planning Interaction (cont.)

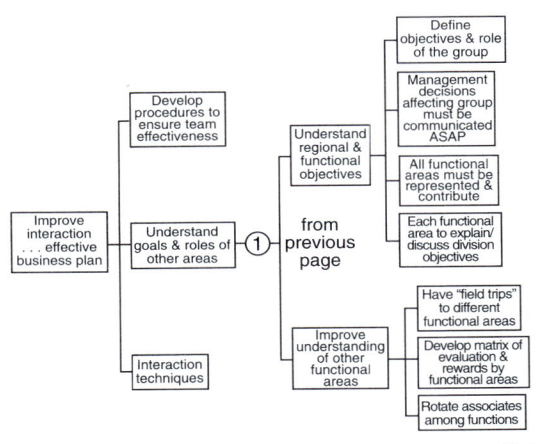

```
Improve interaction ... effective business plan
├── Develop procedures to ensure team effectiveness
├── Understand goals & roles of other areas ──(1)── from previous page
│       ├── Understand regional & functional objectives
│       │       ├── Define objectives & role of the group
│       │       ├── Management decisions affecting group must be communicated ASAP
│       │       ├── All functional areas must be represented & contribute
│       │       └── Each functional area to explain/discuss division objectives
│       └── Improve understanding of other functional areas
│               ├── Have "field trips" to different functional areas
│               ├── Develop matrix of evaluation & rewards by functional areas
│               └── Rotate associates among functions
└── Interaction techniques
```

Information provided courtesy of Goodyear

Voice of the Customer (VOC) Data-Collection System
Understanding customer needs

Why use it?

To identify the key drivers of customer satisfaction. It is only through understanding your customers' thought process while they are making their purchasing decisions and while they are using your products or services that you can effectively design, deliver, and improve them. The term *voice of the customer*, or VOC, is used to describe your customers' needs and their perceptions of the quality of your products or services.

What does it do?

- Properly focuses your improvement project
- Provides data to help you develop appropriate measurements
- Helps the team decide what products and services to offer
- Identifies critical features for those products and services, known as Critical To Quality characteristics, or CTQs
- Provides a baseline measure of customer satisfaction against which to measure improvement
- Identifies the key drivers of customer satisfaction

How do I do it?

1. **Identify your customers and what you need to know about their needs**

   - In a SIPOC (Suppliers, Inputs, Process, Outputs, and Customers) context, a customer is anyone who uses or benefits from the output of your process.
     - One of your customers is the next step that occurs in a process after the process delivers an output.
     - Only your customer can define what a defect is.
   - In a marketing context, the term *customer* is usually restricted to the people and groups outside an organization who purchase and/or use a company's products or services.
   - Ask yourself the following questions:
     - What are the outputs of our process? Who are the customers of that output?
     - Are there particular groups of customers whose needs are especially important to our organization?

   Tip You must decide which of the above definitions of *customer* makes more sense for your project. Often it helps to use both definitions—that is, you work primarily with the people involved with the next process step, but you check to ensure that their needs are consistent with the needs of the final customer. Keep in mind the following points:

   - The final customer, or end user, might be far removed from your particular job, but their needs are still important to you (and to everyone else in your organization).
   - You might have multiple customers (and thus multiple needs to consider).

©2002 GOAL/QPC   **Voice of the Customer (VOC) 259**

- If you work on administrative processes, your customers might include your suppliers. For example, a supervisor who supplies you with information that you incorporate into a report for him/her is your customer.

Tip As you work to identify your customers, check with your sponsor(s) and your marketing staff to see if there are large or influential customers whom you should make sure not to overlook.

Tip Often there is no single VOC. Different customers or types of customers usually have different needs and priorities. You should include a wide variety of customers in your initial customer-research efforts. Different types of customers are often referred to as *market segments*.

- Decide what you need to know about your customers.
  - Revisit your charter. What is the purpose of your project?
  - How does this purpose relate to the needs of the customers you have identified? What do you need to know about these customers' needs to make sure your project purpose is on track?

2. **Collect and analyze reactive system data; then fill any gaps with proactive approaches**
   - There are two types of data-collection systems: reactive and proactive.
   - *Reactive* systems involve information that you receive whether or not you take any action to obtain it.
     - Reactive systems are customer-initiated. Some examples are complaints, returns, credits, and warranty claims.

- It is best to start your data-collection process with reactive data because it is usually easier to get and can give you a basic understanding of customer concerns, allowing you to better focus your proactive work.
- Reactive systems generally gather data about the following:
  - Current and former customer issues or problems.
  - Current and former customers' unmet needs.
  - Current and former customers' interest in particular products or services.

Tip Sometimes customers communicate with you when they have a problem, but other times they let their behavior do the talking. Also, they often don't think of a problem they have as a problem that your organization can solve. Rather, they might blame themselves for the product or service not working right, think they have the wrong product or service, or simply take their business elsewhere. Reactive systems help you capture all the ways in which customers communicate their needs.

Tip It is important to explore this often-underused source of information before making an effort to gather new information. You can learn a great deal about improving your existing products and services if you put extra effort into categorizing and analyzing data from reactive systems and reviewing them periodically to identify patterns, trends, and other opportunities.

Tip Feedback from customers is easily lost. Extra effort must be made to preserve as much of this information as possible.

- *Proactive* systems involve taking action to gather information.
  - Proactive systems are not customer-initiated. Some examples are market research, customer interviews, and surveys.
  - Follow up on the information you obtain to expand your understanding of your customers' needs and to quantify the importance they place on various product/service characteristics.

  Tip Proactive systems are those in which you initiate contact with customers. Ideally, they involve some face-to-face interviews or customer-site visits. Typically they also involve telephone interviews or surveys and/or questionnaires that customers fill out and return to your organization.

  Tip You will likely have to design and initiate targeted customer contact to gather information specifically related to your project. Look for ways to integrate your efforts with ongoing customer contact done by your organization. For example, request that customer service or marketing staff ask additional questions during their regular contacts with customers, or see if your customers will allow you to observe their workplace during a scheduled visit.

3. **Analyze the data you collect to generate a key list of customer needs in their language. Much of this data will be verbal. It is helpful to summarize this information in a meaningful way, perhaps by using an Affinity Diagram.**

4. **Use an Affinity Diagram, a CTQ Tree, and the Kano Model to prioritize the CTQs for your project**

y = f (x) Formula
Identifying the key process drivers

Why use it?

To determine what factors in your process (as indicated by a measure) you can change to improve the CTQs—and, ultimately, the key business measures.

What does it do?

- Illustrates the causal relationship among the key business measures (designated as Y), the process outputs directly affecting the Y's (designated as CTQ or y), and the factors directly affecting the process outputs (designated as x)
- Enables members of your improvement team to communicate the team's findings to others in a simple format
- Highlights the factors the team wants to change and what impact the change will have
- Provides a matrix that can be used in the Control step of the DMAIC method for ongoing monitoring of the process after the team's improvement work is complete

A Causal Relationship

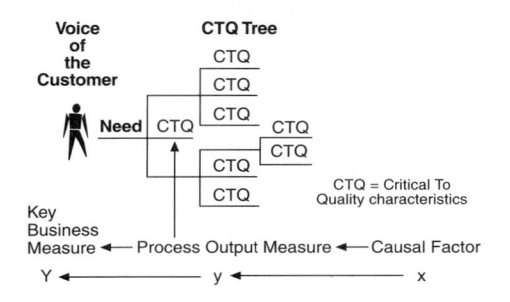

Voice of the Customer — **CTQ Tree**

```
                    CTQ
                    CTQ
                    CTQ
         Need  CTQ
                    CTQ
                    CTQ
                    CTQ
```

CTQ = Critical To Quality characteristics

Key Business Measure ← Process Output Measure ← Causal Factor

Y ← y ← x

Many people understand the concept of $y = f(x)$ from mathematical education. The x, y, Y matrix is based on this concept. If it confuses team members to use these letters, simply use the terms *key business measures*, *CTQ* or *process outputs*, and *causal factors* instead; they represent the same concepts.

How do I do it?

1. **Gather the key business measures for your project (see the team charter or check with your sponsor)**

2. **Gather the CTQs that the improvement team selects as the most important for your project**

3. **List the key business measure and the CTQ operational definition in a matrix, like the one on the next page**

4. **As your team progresses through the Measure and Analyze steps of the DMAIC method, add the causal-factor definitions (x's) you discover**

   Tip When filling out the matrix, use the guidelines in the table shown on page 266 for assistance.

264 $y = f(x)$ Formula

A Sample x, y, Y Matrix

	Y	y	x
Example 1	Revenue: Percentage of revenue from new accounts	Percentage of credit applications approved late	Elapsed time from receipt of all documentation to decision being made
Example 2	Expenses: Timeliness	Percentage of questions not resolved the first time	Percentage of questions not in "Frequently Asked Questions" guide Uptime on the computer system

Guidelines for Filling Out an x, y, Y Matrix

	Y →	→ y →	→ x
What Is Being Measured	Indicators of how the overall organization is performing and of where improvement and innovation need to take place.	Measures of primary interest to the customer or business; how a defect relates to the customer's CTQ measurements.	Measures of importance to the process and the workers, but of little direct importance to the customer.
How Used	Used to make strategic business decisions and to allocate resources.	Used to assess how well the process is performing, where improvement and innovation need to take place, and how the performance of this process relates to the Y's.	Used as tactical day-to-day levers to influence y and Y and to focus improvement teams as needed.
Timing	• Lagging indicator of y (i.e., you will see movement in the Y variable after the y variable has moved). • Note: Time lag might be short or long depending on your measurement system.	• Lagging indicator of x (i.e., you will see movement in the y variable after the x has moved). • Leading indicator of Y (i.e., you will see movement in the y variable before you see change in the Y). • Note: Time lag might be short or long depending on your measurement system.	• Leading indicator of y (i.e., you will see movement in the y variable after you see change in the x variable).
How Measured	Expressed as actual performance.	Can be expressed as a sigma score comparing a customer's or business's requirements to the actual performance.	Can be expressed as a sigma score comparing an in-process requirement to the actual performance.

266 y = f (x) Formula   ©2002 GOAL/QPC